MAKE $#IT HAPPEN

MAKE $#IT HAPPEN

How to be a charismatic client magnet,
double your fees, work with celebrities,
Fortune 500's and millionaires

From the Director of Million Dollar Branders

JUSTINE POGROSKE

First Printing: 2017
ISBN 978-0-646-97724-9

Publishers

PHOENIX
PUBLISHING HOUSE
WWW.PHOENIXPUBLISHINGHOUSE.COM

MILLION DOLLAR BRANDERS
GLOBAL HEAD OFFICE | SYDNEY | AUSTRALIA
Address: 100 Harris St, Sydney NSW, 2009
Phone: +612 8007 6671

Connect with Million Dollar Branders

(f) **milliondollarbranders**

(IG) **milliondollarbranders**

(in) **milliondollarbranders**

(YouTube) **milliondollarbranders**

DEDICATION

To all the entrepreneurs and dreamers who don't eat or sleep before the job is done... always pushing to learn more, to do better, to achieve higher... this book is for you.

CONTENTS

FORWARD

The lesson behind success is to harness opportunity, let go of the outcome and embrace the uncertainty of life. There are pivotal moments in the human life cycle—from birth to death—which are trials and tribulations born from a mindset that fears being controlled. The entrepreneurial heart beats with the initiative to seize the opportunity from a young age and the resilience to achieve at all costs, with hindsight that there is a pot of gold at the end of the rainbow. Seeking opportunity through this journey and self –assurance of the journey are what lead to a complete ending.

Justine Pogroske's words speak to the true heart of the entrepreneur, no holds barred and not sugar-coated. This is what it takes to seal the deal. Her insights are so straight edged and it reminds me—even after more than fifteen years of entrepreneurial struggle and success—of why we choose to go it alone and why the adrenaline fuelled by success is so invigorating. Through inflicting a humour she reminds us of how occasionally we choose to merely express or remain inactive, rather than making $#IT happen.

Every success story has a great beginning and that begins with acknowledging our own value. Our badge of honour is wearing our heart on our sleeve and taking ownership for our unwavering resilience to fulfilling our need to succeed, our intoxicating passion and our spirited exuberance to want to work with like-minded creatives, and the importance of learning to balance success with sustainability. For the flow of life is a constant that we need to remind ourselves is a precious commodity, perhaps even more so than the time and determination we need to ensure longevity...to endure and succeed.

The undeniable understanding that some people exist and are determined to siphon every last drop of their ambition while others merely drain is what strengthens the entrepreneurial spirit on all the lessons of life's journey and what they leave on us. This is what motivates us to overcome challenges rather than corral us.

My name...
My brand...
My persistence...
My initiative...
My vision...
My all...

These are the credentials for success, tabled with succinct accuracy and process. The rest, as they say, is up to you.

Andrew Marcello Morello
"Living the Dream"

ABOUT ANDREW MORELLO

Andrew Morello, winner of the first season of The Apprentice Australia, credits his strong work ethic as the catalyst for his success. Morello's lifelong exposure to the property and finance industry, natural enthusiasm and outstanding sales skills means he is adept at providing people with the service and outcome they are seeking.

A natural leader from his days at St Bernard's College, Morello founded his own business at the age of fifteen and never looked back. Morello is now Head of Business Development at Yellow Brick Road and is working closely with Executive Chairman Mark Bouris to further grow Yellow Brick Road's expanding branch network. Morello is also the co-founder of online jewellery company Bellagio and Co. and a founding member of The Entourage, Australia's largest educator and community of entrepreneurs with over 85,000 members around the world.

Morello's number one mantra is that relationships are the key to a lifetime of success.

ABOUT JUSTINE POGROSKE

"*Justine Pogroske is a master at establishing and amplifying brands.*"
New York Journal

Justine started her first business at age 6 and never looked back. She is now a branding expert and global keynote speaker who helps companies and brands accelerate their success. She is masterful at showing entrepreneurs and driven individuals how hustle, disruption, creativity, passion, and innovation lead to transformation and excellence.

Over the past decade Justine has emerged as a creative visionary and futurist in the advertising, creative, and digital industry. She began her career working for top global advertising and digital agencies. Through this time, Justine had the opportunity to work and learn alongside some of the best creative directors and talent in the world.

The time for Justine to pursue her own avenue came and she founded the global advertising agency, Million Dollar Branders. Her agency focuses on building smaller brands and turning them into million dollar empires, as well as taking big brands and accelerating their success even further to be game changers in their industries.

Justine has worked with celebrities, millionaires, Fortune 500 companies, leading tech start ups, top venture capitalists and global brand giants such as Coke, American Express, Nike, Optus, PwC and Qantas.

When asked to describe her Million Dollar Branders team, Justine says, *"We are the crazy ones, the dreamers, the doers, movers, and shakers, innovators and misfits, the rebels who break rules and challenge conventions. We don't do things the usual way, we challenge companies and brands and how they are perceived, we give them an emotive hook and creative raving fans in a fast moving world. We are not just branders, we are game changers."*

Justine is also featured in a series that has taken the internet by storm called *"THE MILLION DOLLAR ELEVATOR PITCH"* hosted on their YouTube channel *MILLION DOLLAR BRANDERS*. In this series Justine interviews the best of the best: entrepreneurs, millionaires, technopreneurs, thought leaders, innovators, global leaders, hustlers, futurists, fashion icons, movers, shakers, CEOs, and world changers—all in an actual elevator! It's an ideal show for achievers to better understand how being a driven visionary with a million dollar mindset, drive, perseverance and the right attitude can cement the brightest future.

She and her team have also created an educational program called *"THE MILLION DOLLAR SQUAD"*— the program embraces lost young talent, entrepreneurs, futurists and visionaries who need experience—preparing them for the real world. These young-guns are given a platform and program where they can unleash their creative, entrepreneurial business minds and contribute toward building million dollar empires and making $#it happen in the world on a larger scale.

Justine's internationally sought out keynote presentation *"MAKE $#IT HAPPEN"* is shifting mindsets around the world. She inspires people to live with purpose, passion and fulfill their dreams.

If you would like to find out how to get Justine to visit your city and inspire at your event email her at:
bookings@milliondollarbranders.com

WHEN PEOPLE ASK, "WHAT DO YOU DO," TELL THEM "WHATEVER IT TAKES."

With a vast world filled with many resources, entrepreneurs and innovators need to be smart about what they vest their time in. They must know that their business investments are working optimally to create exceptional distinction. The goal should be to strive for a million dollar brand, and beyond.

Your brand is everything to you in your world. If you have goals, you need a personal brand, and if you have ideas they need to be branded so they reach the people they are intended for. Your brand is the legacy you leave behind.

In MAKE $#IT HAPPEN Justine Pogroske shares what you need to know, more than what you may want to hear. If you're serious about developing the habits and practices to brand yourself and your business, you'll appreciate that all the crap is cut. The focus is on what you can do, what you need to do.

Justine Pogroske is an internationally acclaimed branding expert, keynote speaker, and the Founder and Director of Million Dollar Branders, a renowned global advertising agency that is notorious for building million dollar brands.

ACKNOWLEDGEMENTS

This book is from my heart, created with all the heart and passion I have to muster.

To "my sky, stars and lion"— the one that uplifts me and helps me grow every day I am alive, I love you eternally. Thank you for encouraging me on my journey to become who I am today and to relentlessly pursue all of my dreams.

Thank you to my family—
my dad, Trevor—who I thank for inheriting your incredible work ethic. Thank you a million times for all the sacrifices you made for all three of us to live a better life.
my mom, Anne—the qualities go on and on—you are a super woman who I admire in every single way, you have never stopped giving emotionally, physically and mentally to be there for me through good times and bad. You have always been my driving force and my bond with you is one I cherish with all my heart. Thank you for saying "you can" when I thought "I couldn't" you are at the heart of everything I do.
My sister—Loren. You have always believed in me, even with my certain level of crazy. I have always looked up to you for your natural ability to make people laugh, your beauty and amazing family values. It has made all the difference. I love you more than life.
My baby brother, Dean, your business smarts, and street smarts are skills that I admire, you are my best friend forever. Thank you for your support and belief in me always. You continue to teach me every day. I am so grateful for everything you do for me. I adore you.
My nephews—Aiden, Jonny-bear and Giddy - your smarts and pureness always teach me the beauty of life through new eyes. I adore you, may your success be untapped as you reach beyond the clouds.
My second mothers— who brought me up in Africa - Orpa and Marie, Thank you for teaching me discipline, tenacity and humbleness. I love you with all my heart. I am so grateful to you for teaching me the lessons that have made me the woman I am today.

My Million Dollar (Branders) Dream Team—who would I be without you, thank you for believing in my company vision and helping to build a platform to help others succeed. I appreciate you more than you know. You are only as good as the team you work with, and this proves to be true. You are my family. Where I go, you go.

To Simon—the incredible creative director who gave me my first foot in the industry, I am forever grateful. Thank you for recognizing my talent, having the patience to help me build it and for your ability to 'see' and believe in me.

There are some people who taught me what true leadership was - Jonas, James, Mathew and Stuart - thank you for embracing my talent in the wild- west of advertising and always having my back! your talent, humbleness, drive to suceed, and integrity will always be admired by me.

My best friends, my extended family—you know who you are—you have always helped me carry on; fearless in telling me the good, bad, and ugly, helping me to be the best version of myself every single day. You are my greatest reason for being the best version of myself.

Although she looks down at me today my best friend—who I would refer to as my "sister", Amelia, who was stolen from this earth by bowel cancer at the young age of 32, will always be a beautiful part of my life. She was one of the strongest people I've ever known, always able to smile and laugh and make a difference.

Then there is Bobba Lilly, who always encouraged me to be my best self and who never ceased to show me what kindness was from a very young age. You knew I had talent before I even did. Thank you for embracing it.

To God and to the the universe—thank you for making my dreams a reality. My life continues to flow in the most positive light. I am grateful for everything, every day I am on this earth. My promise to you is that I will not rest until I help millions of people realize what they are capable of, and give back just a bit of what you have given me.

"MIRACLES HAPPEN WHEN YOU WORK HARDER ON YOUR DREAMS THAN ON YOUR FEARS. BE FEARLESS. BE BRAVE. YOU HAVE NOTHING TO LOSE."

Justine P.

JUSTINE P. - FOUNDER - MILLION DOLLAR BRANDERS PTY.LTD

INTRODUCTION

'It's all about You

Our modern world moves fast. No opinion or attitude can speed it up or slow it down. But they sure as hell will slow "you" down if you're not in the right mindset. Technology changes lives for the better. It's also a portal that grants access to the world for business executives and entrepreneurs.

This is our world, but the question is: what will you do within it? Some of you will freak out because you lack the confidence to establish yourself in this foreign technological world.

As someone once begged, "Please, for the love of G-d, don't do it!" Don't turn your back to what you should be doing in this life. Be the person who accepts control and takes action. Create the brand of you—because if you can't sell you, no one can.

This book will guide you in gaining the confidence to start a business and build your dream brand from scratch. It will empower you to overcome challenges and keep moving forward. Hopefully it will convince you that anything is possible, and you'll have the strength and insights to know how to make $#IT happen.

> ***Big dreams are rewarded to Big dreamers. It is up to you to work hard on that dream. You need to put all of your heart and soul into making it happen.***

You may be wondering who I am to tell you this. I'm someone who has found success from the lessons shared in this book. I work with people who have fearless visions for their companies as they create a brand. And I effing love it! I am living my dream. I am a million-dollar brand in myself and I want to help you become one too.

The opportunity is in your court. You have this amazing book in your hands, and there is some seriously good $#IT in it. However, I can't make you take action. That, my friend, is up to you. If you're lazy, you'll get results that reflect that. For those of you who know that it's time for action, let's walk through it together.

Much love,

Justine P.

"NOTHING IN LIFE
IS UNATTAINABLE.
LIFE JUST WANTS
YOU TO SHOW IT
HOW BADLY
YOU WANT IT."

Justine P.

JUSTINE P. - FOUNDER - MILLION DOLLAR BRANDERS PTY LTD

THE BOSS MINDSET
Do What it Takes

All life begins with the untouched potential that is instilled within us, from the moment we are born. As we progress though life, we experience specific moments that allow us to grow and develop our inner potential. These specific moments may lead us to finding success, satisfaction, happiness or may even disengage us from the potential that is embedded within our nature.

Regardless of those experiences that may have warped your mindset, good or bad. You need to understand that you have the potential to excel and make your own mark on the world. The Boss Mindset exists within all of us. It is up to you to find it. It's up to you to make $#it Happen.

The strong minded nature of my mother has moulded and inspired me to be the successfully driven person I am today. She allowed me to realize that in order to be successful, you need to see the potential within yourself.

I grew up in Johannesburg, South Africa, and lived a very happy life—until age 11 ½. One Saturday night my father, brother, and I drove to the local video store to pick out a movie. Upon returning home, we drove up our driveway and were in the middle of a shoot out.

There were nine gunmen who were firing from large machine guns, the image still plays on my mind. In the house was my mom, who hid in our bathtub to keep herself from getting shot dead.

The next six weeks were the hard and traumatic. We began packing up our lives and everything we knew that was familiar to us to head toward a brighter future. When we boarded the plane, we headed to the place I've called home since—Sydney, Australia.

My father was still wrapping up his business that he ran in Johannesburg, so my mother took us three kids and began to figure it out. I remember her unpacking a 40' container in an unknown suburb and trying to begin a new life. While Mom cooked and cleaned and took care of us, she also became a full-time psychologist to the whole family. My mom is a saint.

She is a supermom. She never showed that she was breaking, even when I am sure she was many times over. I think this is where I inherited my tenacity and strength from.

> *"When the going gets tough, the tough gets going. You are what you think you are. If you" want something bad enough you'll go out and get it."*
> **– Anne Pogroske** *(Mom)*

Mom has pushed me through some of the lowest points in my life, those moments where I had to decide whether to fade into the shadows or get back to work. You know what I mean; we've all been there at some point. For me, I know this: the difference between me and others is my "never say die" attitude. I am going to win, or die trying.

This "do whatever it takes attitude" did help me through rough times, but my "hustle at all costs" mentality helped me excel. It may be a bold step, but I'd dare say that I was born with it.

At six years old, I started my first business in the backyard of my Johannesburg home. I decided to sell some of the toys I was no longer using for a deeply discounted price. It was highly logical to me in every way. So I commissioned my three and a half year old brother, Dean, in exchange for all of my "contraband" (chocolates, sweets, and a lifetime supply of chewing gum) in lieu of his time. It was my first JV (joint venture) and I made him sign a contract using my green crayon. Then he started work.

We put a sign on the fence that read: "TOY STORE—everything MUST GO!" It was drawn in red and yellow crayon combined with purple highlighter stars, and to our surprise, as workers walked by in the afternoon, they'd eagerly buy dolls and toys from us in bulk to bring home to their children. It was the hottest business in Johannesburg, making me a very powerful six year old reseller and distributor. I had so much money that I was stuffing it in my teddy bears. Mom didn't know what I was doing, and she certainly grew curious about where I was getting my money from. When she found out that I had turned her garden into a one-stop-shop industrial toy-storing-ground she wasn't too happy and shut me down right away. Aside from the toy business, I also started a side hustle—selling fake nails. Yes, fake nails!

After mom's beauty business venture failed I noticed her eagerly throwing away bags and bags of fake nails, pink and purple, silver ones, striped ones. I thought, how could she throw these out? What a waste! It was like throwing money down the toilet! That morning before school, I went and dug them out from the garbage bags, deciding they were my new business treasure!

That day, when the bell rang for break time on my first day of school I set up shop in my school desk where I had a sign: "JUSTINE'S BEAUTY SHOP". I was inundated with new clients—all girls under the age of eight. And I made a killing! Honestly, I had no idea if they really were interested in the nails or just the experience of purchasing them from me OR because it had become a fad. Anyone who was "anyone" had to have these nails! I was the richest first grader in South Africa. Every girl in school walked around strutting their stuff with long fake nails—quite a hilarious site. Then to my surprise, the school principal wasn't so impressed and shut me down. I decided it was time for a career change.

After that came my illustration business, where I created a cartoon animal that was half polar bear and half koala, named "KG". I put my number on a flyer that read: For customized orders please call Justine. And they called. However, Mom answered the phone one day and was a bit surprised to hear an elder woman's voice asking for me NOT her. My orders grew and grew to the stage my mom refused to be my "personal secretary", as she called it. As the orders came through and I drew and drew, my hand pain began—an eight year old can only draw so many sketches in one day. I had back-orders from here to China. Not long after, I came to a serious conclusion—there was too much manual labor involved for a kid my age and I made the executive decision that the business was not scalable so I shut shop.

A few years later, we moved to Australia and things got a little tougher. Let's just start by saying that I am not an academic, never have been and never will be. I did things by taking action. I'd rather work my a$$ off right from the start, and hustle using my street smarts rather than sit in a classroom, only to go out into the "real world" and learn that I still will have to work my a$$ off and play some catch-up, too. This made my last year of school in Australia a tough one for me.

I wanted to go into graphic design after high school, which required that I get an extremely high mark on my high school certificate. It required me to dig down into academics in a way that was highly unpleasing, yet I was determined. I didn't come out of my bedroom for a full year, my REDBULL wall became HUGE. Peoples' doubts drove me, but my amazing mom was helping to positively drive me, as I worked so hard to get that "coveted ranking." In the end, I missed my result by 1%. Ouch! I was devastated.

At my school, it was a shameful thing to attend anything less than a private college. And if you didn't get a mark high enough to do so, well, you were a "dumba$$."

What I did not realize was that by missing my course by less than 1%, I was entering the 1% of people who don't fit into the other

99%ers. Who are we? Who are the 1%ers? We are the movers, the shakers, and the people who fight as hard as we can to make up for the "academic mind" we are missing. We are the 1% who make $#IT happen. While everyone is sleeping, we are working. While others dream, we take action to make our dreams a reality. We do things differently, but certainly no less effectively.

I'd been detoured, but not derailed.

For me, at that moment when I missed "that mark," I knew letting a f'en test tell me what I could and couldn't do was not an option. I had to develop my resilience and find a different way to get to where I wanted to be. I never looked at "no" like a "no," for me a "no" has always been one step closer to a "yes."

Mom was relentless in helping me figure out a path. She sat with me and looked through every single course available to do graphic design. She was not about to give up, and because of that, I knew I would not either. It turned out that luck was on my side! By not getting into a snobby high-end college or having my mommy and daddy bail me out by paying for my marks (as some of the other kids did) it was a blessing in disguise. I received an opportunity to attend a hands-on school specializing in the creative fields known as The Enmore Design Centre.

What was great about Enmore was that they didn't care about money. That wasn't the criterion for getting in. Since I didn't have any, I definitely liked that. Plus, I always believed that money couldn't make someone talented. At Enmore, for entry, you had to take a drawing test and show you had some skill. Now that was something I could prove.

This was so important to me, and Mom was right there, telling me, "Don't give up, don't give up." I could look at her and know with absolute certainty that she meant what she said. I could do it and giving up wasn't going to be an option. It paid off!

Being there was intensive and incredible. I had to work hard, always extending myself to my limits, and some days it seemed like beyond. It was worth it because the hands-on training I received was the exact type of learning that resonated with me best.

By the time I made it through the program and went to work for my first company, a publishing firm that custom designed for twenty-four magazines, with the creative work being done by two of us—my UK Creative Director and myself, I was all in. Like in the deep end, but I learned how to swim—fast. It was a first step towards a great future. Until...

Something awful happened to me—like make my heart drop into my stomach awful. It was 5:30 PM and I was finishing up some things for the publication, which was set to go to print the next morning at 9:00 AM. My Creative Director was the last to leave for the day and waved goodbye as he walked out. Just as he walked out, I accidentally deleted the entire magazine. The entire thing—gone! It was an effin' technology moment, I admit.

I was in tears, fearful of losing my job, and I was still a junior. I was getting good at what I was doing but certainly hadn't arrived. After a call to Mom, she instantly got me to redirect to a more positive line of thinking. She asked me if they had a print-out of the entire magazine that would give me an overview of what editors signed off on. Yes, they did. My thoughts went straight from hopeless to hopeful. Mom was good at always looking at the glass half full.

> *Mom taught me a fundamental lesson at that moment, and that was how to bring back perspective and find my perseverance so I could take action.*

Now we were getting somewhere. Mom drove to my work and sat with me until 4 AM the next morning while I redid the entire magazine. I was solving my big problem, while also gaining a great mother-daughter bonding experience that I will never forget as long as I live. It was a tough and exhausting night, but I refused to make any excuses about why I couldn't do it because the magazine needed to be reconstructed. On a funny note, they say the second-time creative round is always better. It's the truth. The magazine got rave reviews when it came back from print. My small battle had turned into a big win!

It felt great to solve this problem, but as most of us recognize, we are all going to meet our fair share of obstacles at some point when we are throwing ourselves into our dreams and passions. Some obstacles will be big, and some will be little. It happens. You've got to deal with it, learn, and move on.

I'd never really wanted to spend my life laying out other peoples' copy, but it was a good experience to gain. I was always intrigued with advertising, the feeling of watching a great advert on TV or reading a clever advert in a magazine or newspaper with a revealing "aha" moment; there was always a connection. Up to this point, my creative talent was still untapped, and I moved on from "magazine publishing land" to start my love affair with the glamorous world of advertising.

I began to campaign for the opportunity I wanted. For about four weeks, I couriered parcels to the Creative Director that were clever. One example was a pair of baby shoes, saying: "I need to learn to walk before I run, but I promise I will be your best runner. Give me a job...PLEASE!" I was finally offered a job at one of the biggest global ad agencies in Sydney where I worked devotedly for about three years. It was a great three years, and I was surrounded by some of the most brilliant "creatives" in the world.

During my last few months at that job the GFC (global financial crisis) hit. They let go of the talented and encouraging Swedish Creative Director I was working with, made him redundant, and told him not to come back. They also let go of the rock star English deputy Creative Director. This destroyed the agency's morale as a whole.

A few weeks later, the agency put on another Creative Director who was conceited, arrogant, and his head was up in the clouds. He called me into his office and decided to let me know -- after I had worked until 4 AM the previous morning on a Coke campaign --that I didn't quite "fit." He then made a comment that I wasn't worth my junior salary of $25K (beyond insulting), and he didn't know why I was still there after all those years.

He was an idiot. I never personalized this or let it make me weak, though. I definitely thought you're right, actually. I don't know why I'm still here; I am worth way more than $25K. I am worth my weight in gold.

Never define your value by other peoples' beliefs in you.

Little did I know that this value system would lead to the name of my future company: MILLION DOLLAR BRANDERS.

After giving the agency blood, sweat, and tears for three-plus years of my life...well, lack of life because all I did was work, I quit. I knew it was time to get out into the big world and live my true value.

Since then it has been a journey, and I have worked for some of the biggest companies and clients in the world. In my head, I thank that Creative Director every day. If it were not for him, I would probably still be there churning and burning just like everyone else still there, still engulfed in the agency's churning and burning flames.

If we know we're of value, we have to be fearless to show it.

I credit my mom for so much of this strength because she always knew I was destined for things greater, probably even more than I thought at times. Not everyone has my mom in their corner, but what she's taught me is at the heart of Million Dollar Branders and how we conduct business. She taught me strength and perseverance. She taught me what makes up a Million Dollar Brand.

THE PARABLE OF DISTINCTION

This is a story that my mother often told me when I was younger. She wanted me to know that I should always embrace being "different". The story has always stuck with me, and it is a reminder of the beauty of distinction and being comfortable in not being a cookie cutter person in life.

If you attended a party and there was a tray of beautiful white meringues, fluffy and luscious, you'd notice and probably want one. After all, they look amazing. However, in the centre of all those delicious meringues is a single bright pink dusted coconut macaroon. Which one do you pick?

The pink coconut macaroon is a one of a kind, not a mould that does what society expects it should be—it is comfortable as it is. When it comes to people, you don't want to be one meringue on the platter filled with them, you want to be the macaroon!

I go through life embracing that I'm a macaroon and I'm comfortable with it. I don't have to be smarter than everyone else; I just have to know who to surround myself with to lift myself up. I'm a creative, not an academic, and that is great by me. And it serves my clients and life well.

Back in high school when I was bullied for my uniqueness, it bothered me at times. They called me "dumb." I called it disinterested. My aspirations were different.

There was a difference between me and them. A teacher could fail me for whatever their reason. Maybe they're having a bad day, and that's fine, but it can never take away what I know about me: I can do this. This is the way everyone should view their world. Others' opinions don't need to be your damn business, really. You've got to have a strong mindset.

Not everyone gets it earlier in life. I recall seeing a guy that was in my art classes. He was so talented - by far, the best artist in our class. Our teacher picked on him incessantly and told him he wasn't anything special. He finally believed her because he dropped out three months before graduation.. I ran into him years later, packing boxes at a warehouse store, and asked him what the hell he was doing. He said he wasn't cut-out for art.

Outside influences shouldn't define who we are.

You will serve yourself well to commit to not being one of those "I wish I'd done that" types of people. You know, one of the many meringues on the plate.

"The graveyard is the richest place on earth, because it is here that you will find all the hopes and dreams that were never fulfilled, the books that were never written, the songs that were never sung, the inventions that were never shared, the cures that were never discovered, all because someone was too afraid to take that first step, keep with the problem, or determined to carry out their dream."

–Les Brown

Every hour of every minute of every day is valuable. Make the most of it. Everyone is capable of making $#it happen.

MAKE $#IT HAPPEN CHECKLIST

✔ **Watch your self-talk:** Be your own 'biggest fan'. You can't tap your full potential if you downplay yourself. Always back yourself.

✔ **Eliminate negative energy:** Negative people are problems because you will become negative. Move these creativity killers aside. You don't need them.

✔ **Guard your environment:** Putting yourself in a negative environment can effect your success dramatically. No matter how positive you are, a negative environment can rub off on you until your mind unintentionally resorts to negative thoughts before positive ones. Watch your space.

✔ **Have Balance:** You can't gain quality results in your life if you give everything toward your work and nothing toward your health and personal life. Oppositely, you cannot just focus on having fun personally and expect to grow professionally. Walk the line of balance.

✔ **Action your dreams:** Dreams are time wasters if you are not going to put them into action. Don't waste your time dreaming big- if you're head's going to remain in the clouds and your feet are never pounding the pavement.

"YOU ARE RESPONSIBLE FOR ALL THE OPPORTUNITIES IN YOUR LIFE CREATE THEM - PASSIONATELY."

Justine P.

JUSTINE P. - FOUNDER - MILLION DOLLAR BRANDERS

OWN YOUR PERSONAL POWER
You've Got To Connect with Your Super Self

One of the most important lessons that I've learned as a Brand Specialist is to embrace *myself*. Particularly, my...

- Differences
- Focus
- Competition
- Distinctions

If you go through your day talking a big game, but not having the internal conviction to back it up, you're going to be—screwed. There is no way to put that delicately. And you should be grateful to hear it directly, not in some round-about way that you don't really catch on to. Precision does matter.

I've worked with a ridiculously high number of clients since branching off to do business the way that I felt it could be done (successfully). Using my personal power to connect with clients is only the start of how I can serve them best. You must know the client before you can help them craft their vision successfully.

There is nothing that gives you more of a professional buzz than taking a failing or misguided brand ideal and flipping it on its ear.

When a business goes from playing in the minor leagues to being a million-plus dollar business in the major leagues, it leaves an impression. The brand becomes distinct and undeniable.

Through all of this, I've learned an over-arching lesson that applies to every entrepreneur or person who seeks distinction: people are buying people. *You* are important. *You* are your brand. It truly is all about you.

But you need tenacity!

According to research on sales by Marketing Donut[1], the art of getting people to "buy you" requires tenacity. Yeah, you basically need it as much as oxygen. The research indicates:

- *44% of sales people give up after one "no."*
- *22% give up after two "no's."*
- *14% give up after three "no's."*
- *12% give up after four "no's."*

  That tells you that 92% of sales people give up after four "no's," and only 8% cent of sales people ask for the order a fifth time.

When you consider that 80% of prospects say "no" four times before they say "yes," the inference is that 8% of sales people are getting 80% of the sales.

Do you get where I'm going with this? It tells a picture that's bigger than how you may envision your typical salesman. When it comes to you, do you have the tenacity you need to remain standing long after everyone moves on to their next rejection?

You've got to go face-to-face with people to really get great sales results. From my experience I've learnt that it's the initial face-to-face interaction with my prospective clients that seals the deal. They are buying me. They know, like and trust me. They are confident I will deliver them the results they need. I am bold in my approach and unapologetic. You can't be a mouse in the room, hiding in its bolt hole and expect to get results. Get out there! A lot of people give up just before they are about to succeed or have a major break-through. Don't be one of these people.

> **Small minds can't comprehend big spirits. To be great, you have to be willing to be mocked, hated, and misunderstood. You have to stay strong.**

So how do you become the best of the best? For a start, you need to work out your WHY. Your WHY will always fuel your fire, even when times are tough. What is it that makes you tick? What are your strengths? Your weaknesses? What drives you to get out of bed in the morning? What are you truly good at?. What are you "known for". What is a skill or talent you have that no-one around you has?

These factors and qualities will help you to define your personal power. Success is earned, but knowing your WHY will drive you when others are falling away and giving up.

I know that I am willing to outwork everyone I need to in order to achieve what I've set to do, or I'll die trying. I have never assumed that I will be successful. I know it's effin' earned. My passion for digital advertising began when I saw how powerful the medium could be, and realized that I was willing to do something that others have begun to think of as awkward—talk to people in order to help them create digital branding that is authentic and results driven. I constantly research, mastering everything I need to know. Most people don't do that. What I've learned will never be learned in school or a seminar. It's me keeping my nose to the grindstone and my eyes on the prize.

What is that dream you say you're ready for? What have you done so far so achieve it? How far are you willing to go to get it? A person who makes $#it happen is in it for the long haul. *Are you ready to make $#it happen?* If you are, I can assure you it is worth the hard work.

MAKE $#IT HAPPEN CHECKLIST

✔ **Drop the excuses**: If things aren't getting done, if you aren't moving forward, you've got to look at what you're doing, not what everyone else is trying to stop you from doing. Have tunnel vision.

✔ **Your success is up to you**: Here's a news flash for you—most people don't want you to become more successful than they are. If you rely on what they say, you might as well let them be your boss.

✔ **The "people factor"**: Step up to the plate, be the most authentic, confident version of yourself. Then hit it out of the park. This will distinguish you from a minor league player to a major league player.

✔ **Drop the laziness**: If you want it, you'll work for it every day. Tirelessly.

✔ **Don't box yourself in**: Experience and educate yourself on different cultures so you can burst through any barrier or stereotype you might encounter. In today's fast paced world, this is important, especially in sales.

WHEN PEOPLE ASK "WHAT DO YOU DO," TELL THEM "WHATEVER IT TAKES."

Justine P.

JUSTINE P. - FOUNDER - MILLION DOLLAR BRANDERS PTY.LTD

DO THE WORK; GET THE RESULTS

Assuming is for Slugs

Mistakes...I can't stand them. But I've made a lot, mostly from being a trusting and warm person. I literally have no mental power to evaluate why someone would say one thing and do another. It makes no sense to me, and it's left me vulnerable a time or two—like a wounded animal with vultures circling around it. Waiting...waiting...waiting.

But I learned quickly.

You don't want to be a vulture, but you sure as hell don't want to be a wounded animal, either. When it comes to dealing with people, do a bit of due diligence and do the work before you jump in the hopper of collaboration with them.

First, Google them and find out about them. It's very rare to meet someone that wants to achieve something professionally that does not have a presence on the internet. Check it all out. Leverage out the good, the bad, and the neutral using some common sense.

Then ask yourself:

- Can I learn from them?
- Will they help me grow?
- Will they add value to my business?
- Do they have what it takes (tenacity, drive, perseverance) to build a million-dollar company?
- Are they open to growing together?

You want to work with people who are smarter than you. Now, this doesn't mean that they are necessarily the C-Suite level employees. It means they've invested time from their lives to master certain things that can help you. And if you're doing it right, other people are going to look to you as the smarter one in the room, too. If not now—eventually, assuming that you are doing what you have to do to become *that* person.

> ***"If you're the smartest person in your group, then you need a new group."***
> **–Les Brown**

If we're serious about reaching our potential, we cannot do it without challenging ourselves. It can be done. It's not impossible to conquer your resistance to a good challenge.

Every single day I do one thing with the specific purpose of growing smarter or better because of it. It's non-negotiable for me. Before I started Million Dollar Branders, I knew a developer that I wanted to work with. The words I thought to describe them were "creative

DO THE WORK; GET THE RESULTS

and edgy"—an unusual skill set for a developer to have as they are usually very technical NOT creative. I thought I'd learn so much.

When the opportunity came to work with this individual, I jumped in without thinking twice. I'd made my assessment. The deposit was paid to us from a big client, and I allowed him to take the entire portion of it, agreeing to get paid at the end, as I knew he was struggling financially. He was grateful, thrilled really. Then he apparently invested in some running shoes, because he took off faster than you can imagine, running away from me, the project, and it turns out, the law too.

What was my mistake? I didn't do my due diligence. Needless to say, this has never happened to me since that time. Lesson learned. Wisdom gained. It was time to move on to opportunities that could actually bring value.

You must think beyond the norm and use your intuition. A desire to work with someone that isn't well thought out (aka researched) is going to bring you some surprises—most of them unpleasant like that pile of crap you accidentally step in on the sidewalk when you're not paying attention.

> *Even between friends, you must*
> *use business standards before*
> *you work with them on projects.*
> *If you don't, there is no faster way*
> *to ruin a friendship and a business*
> *opportunity.*

You can have a business focus and still like the people you work with. Some call it the best of both worlds, but I see it as a result of doing the work. When you do the work, you can even like and admire your competition.

So, what do you do about the competition, anyway?

In terms of business, you've got to know your competition. A lot of people make the mistake of investing their own money in branding, websites, marketing, etc. They don't bother to test their product in the market and get that valuable and very necessary feedback. Then what happens? They don't make a single sale. They've invested a ton of their money, maybe some of their friends and families' monies, as well, and there is nothing good to show for it.

What does this bring you back to? Work with people who are smarter than you. These are the people who've done what you are trying to do before. Find them! Interview the best people in the industry. There is no need to reinvent what exists. You can use the foundation of it to begin. Because, you can emulate existing success, and be an original too. You'll just want to make sure you have the right legal contracts in place to protect you, and them.

> *Whether you're branding a product or yourself, it's the same formula. People buy the experience and emotions. They buy a story before buy stuff and things.*

If you are not smart enough to do the research, find the right people to do it. Whether you want to do it or not doesn't change what needs to be done. Know this:

- Get to know your personal strengths and weaknesses, so you can best serve your growth
- Never be lazy
- Remember, the world is at your fingertips, which means there are no excuses

You can do anything—zero to up. When my family emigrated from South Africa when I was little it was not easy. We had nothing! I went to school five days a week, I had to work and got teased at school because I wasn't like the other kids.

They played, and I worked. I worked in a donut shop and had to do all the clean-up work—including underneath the fridge. Always a disgusting experience, but it taught me a lot about what I wanted to do and what I was willing to do to go for it. You've got to know how to hustle and punch it when you must.

Your life is a gift, own it! Your success lies in your own hands.

All of the best games and sports need a psychological and physical strategy and mindset to succeed. Whether it's playing chess or sailing your boat on the windy ocean, you've got to have discipline and mental toughness, perseverance. Otherwise, you'll never get better at the game. Lackluster efforts create dismal results. You can't be short-sighted.

MAKE $#IT HAPPEN CHECKLIST

✔ **Do your R&D**: Don't be lazy. Do your research and development. Make Google your best friend. What you don't know you can find.

✔ **Have solid resources**: The world consists of millions of people who can help. You can easily gain access to resources which will enable you to smash out your business goals.

✔ **Sound intuition**: Some people are not well-connected with their intuition, which sucks! It's very helpful for making better decisions quickly. If your intuition isn't good, find someone who has been there/done that, and ask them about it.

✔ **Never assume**: You are going to set yourself up for unnecessary frustration if you assume that people will do what you want them to do, or that they will share in your excitement.

✔ **Invest in your due diligence**: If you need to pay for due diligence, PAY. This is no time to be a cheap-skate. And if you don't have the money now—budget for it. This may seem expensive now but it will save you long term. Look for the best Accountants, Insurance, Lawyers and Resources. A strong foundation is fundamental to the future success of your company.

"BE YOUR OWN
COMPETITION."

Justine P.

BE YOUR OWN COMPETITION
Self Motivate

Loads of people are relentless on themselves, when it comes to what they've messed up on. Far too few are relentless on themselves when it comes to being their own competition. To me, this means not looking at what anyone else is doing, but what I'm doing.

In my industry when people ask me what I do, and I share that I'm in digital, their responses are often typical and lame. I hear things like: "That's hard to do." "That is such a competitive industry." Blah-de-effin-blah!

It doesn't matter what you decide to do. There is always going to be thousands of experts. This means you need to learn to embrace the differences in your personality (Your Personal Power) and then market yourself differently.

For me, I'm lucky because
I'm crazy and creating my distinction
comes naturally.

However, if you can't do what needs to be done, you'd better find someone else you trust that can. Being bold and honest may sometimes feel uncomfortable, but you've got to do it if you are vested in results just as much as earning an income.

When I am meeting with potential clients, I don't try to be all things to them. I am who I am and show what I can do that's different. Some love it and are excited; others are not.

> *If someone wants cookie cutter,*
> *they don't want me. And to be honest,*
> *I don't want them.*

I'm not scared about how many digital advertising agencies are out there. Million Dollar Branders wants to make a difference. We want people to research us, and we are definitely going to research them and ask the tough questions. The more people doing business together know each other's professional history and the expectations for the project, the better off we all are.

Are you wondering what happens if you don't have all the answers? Be willing to research and find them out—and then relay the information. I don't know about you, but if I am face-to-face with someone who believes they know all the answers, I'm not buying it. Or should I say, "I'm not buying them."

> *It's your difference and what you can*
> *do that is your brand.*

Are you really good at talking to people? If this is your strength, the muscle from that will let you effortlessly converse with whoever you're sitting next to in a room. You'll stick out by using this strength. It's a tough skill to develop if it doesn't come naturally, so be grateful for what does. Not everything will.

Don't play small—ever! Go big or go home, whether you're at a coffee shop, at home, or in the office. Be a perfectionist and if you are not one, find one. If you're not a systems person, find one. Don't make lame, lazy a$$ excuses for things you can control.

Fearing competition is wasted energy.

Are you obsessed with others? It does not matter what others are doing, whether it's nothing at all or they are busting their a$$es to get $#IT done. You cannot control *that*. You can control *you*.

Focus on your own strengths. When you place so much of your energy in what others are doing, you are likely to go down a negative path that will lead to nothing exciting or beneficial to you. Being genuine along with disciplined cannot be overrated.

Whether you're spiritual or not, know this: the universe is always paying attention. When we give someone a compliment and then wish for their destruction in that same breathe, we are setting ourselves up for a cosmic failure. Implosion!

For example, if someone is a better brander than me, should I hope she has a crap life and rolls around in mud, what good does that do? It shows my weakness, first of all, which makes my stomach flip. But additionally, it's basically saying that I am envious of their success, that I want something bad to happen. These are not the thoughts of a successful person or an achiever. Have you ever heard of the Evil Eye? Look it up, and you'll find endless references to how this type of dour thinking defines your path—and it's not a pleasant one.

When you're thinking, do well, but not too well, you are wasting time and energy on stupid stuff. Personally, I'm well past giving a crap about what anyone says about me. You should do the same. The people in your life to pay attention to are the ones who want you to excel beyond your wildest dreams and will push you through good and bad, doing so even if the truth hurts.

> *You can't care what people think or say. When they are not talking about you, then you have something to worry about.*

Speaking of wasting time... It's a huge epidemic that's bludgeoning countless peoples' potential on a regular basis. Just process this[2]...

- **We spend 25 years sleeping on average if we live to be 75:** Yeah, we need sleep, but the world keeps moving while we sleep. Good to remember...

- **We spend more than 5 year's and 4 month's of our lives on social media:** We spend way to much time worrying about what others are doing, instead of worrying about what our next step is. The average amount of time spent on major social media networks per day include: Facebook (35 min's), Snapchat (25 min's), Instagram (15 min's), Youtube (40 min's) and Twitter (1 hour).

- **We spend 1 year picking out clothes:** The right clothes can define your brand. A little organization can go a long way with this one! This stat does not include shopping time, by the way.

- **We spend 4.3 years of our life driving:** Is drive time productive time? Brainstorm, listen to information to learn, do anything besides zoning out. Occasional rants at bad drivers still okay!

- **We spend 3.6 years eating:** Food, glorious food! Make it satisfying and delicious and the right type of fuel to do everything else you need to do. After all, you can't dump sugar into your car's engine and have it purr like a kitten as it roars down the highway of success.

- **We spend 9 years watching TV:** Yeah, there's some great stuff on TV, but there's also some pretty lousy crap, too. If you are in front of the TV daydreaming about your goals, it's time to shut off the box that's holding you captive and work on achieving something more exciting. How many times do you need to watch a rerun?

- **We spend 10.3 years working:** At least it's higher than TV, I suppose. This assumes a 40-hour work week, though, and that is highly unlikely if you really are serious about making $#IT happen in your life—at least not right away. And don't forget the passion factor. When you love what you do, work is play.

Be honest with yourself. If you know you're wasting time, commit to stopping. Envision what can happen with the better use of your time on all levels of your life. Time is one of the most valuable things we have as human beings. Some say "wasted time is worse than wasted money".

"Now when I was 15 years old, I had a very important person in my life come to me and say, 'who's your hero?' And I said, 'I don't know, I gotta think about that. Give me a couple of weeks.' I come back two weeks later, this person comes up and says, 'who's your hero?' I said, 'I thought about it. You know who it is? It's me in 10 years.'

"So I turned 25. Ten years later, that same person comes to me and says, 'So, are you a hero?' And I was like, 'not even close. No, no, no.' She said, 'Why?' I said, 'Because my hero's me at 35.'

"So you see every day, every week, every month and every year of my life, my hero's always 10 years away. I'm never gonna be my hero. I'm not gonna attain that. I know I'm not, and that's just fine with me because that keeps me with somebody to keep on chasing."

–Matthew McConaughey

I love how McConaughey talked about this in his Oscar acceptance speech. We cannot deny that he's successful, of course, and he also appears to be one of those guys who is comfortable in his own skin. He realizes no one can beat him beside himself. We all need to realize this!

THE DIGITAL INDUSTRY

It always surprises me to see how much poor competition pops up that I actually have to address with people in some manner. The digital industry is massive, after all. Everywhere we look we see "cheap and affordable" digital products. $5 logos, free websites, etc. Have you ever thought about the concept of getting what you pay for? Value added services to grow business usually aren't free, and why would they be? Value-adding services in the business world do come with a price.

You have to have confidence that you are the competitor of choice for any client that you'd like to work with. So, when someone asks me why I charge what I do, my response is simple.

> *When you work with me, you're paying for an expert. You're paying for my intellectual property and my ideas.*

Ideas equal currency. What do you want your ideas to be? You determine it with what you invest and pay for.

It may not be pretty, but it is psychologically valuable. You need to get inside people's head through an image, a slogan. What I share with these people applies to any career that you are in—no exceptions. Are you going to be the basement bargain or the expert that gets $#it done? The thought leader. The last one standing on a pedestal when the fancy lights go off.

When you're in competition with yourself, you are more aware of how you control everything. You learn to get over it...

- Get over the hurdles
- Get over the people who are threatened by you
- Get over people who will always be up against you
- Step into power suit, stand up and take control

Learn what makes you tick because that will ultimately drive you to be the best. Be productive in everything that you do and stop wasting time on the wrong things.

You don't have time to complain when you are in a competition with yourself to become better.

MAKE $#IT HAPPEN CHECKLIST

✔ **Don't give a $#IT about what anyone else is doing**: Remember, while you are too busy looking at everyone else, someone faster, better stronger is out there at the exact same time as you building their million dollar vision and empire and making $#it happen. Be focused and have tunnel vision. You don't have time to waste.

✔ **Find your personal power/ talent that accelerates your success**: Determine your passions and learn how to infuse them into what you do..... this lead to the big bux $$$$$!

✔ **Accept that challenges come with being good**: Channel others envy in a good way. Walk the walk and talk the talk. Be bigger and better.

✔ **Be around the best**: When you are around the best, you will become the best. Environment is everything; I don't like hanging out with people that don't make me grow or become richer mentally.

✔ **Be a master at your skills and job**: Be willing to put in what it takes. You can't have a million-dollar dream with a minimum wage work ethic.

"YOUR SUCCESS
IS DEFINED BY YOU.

YOU WORK FOR IT.
YOU DEFINE IT.
YOU CREATE IT.

LIVE A LIFE
YOU'RE PROUD
TO LIVE.

NOTHING ELSE
MATTERS."

Justine P.

JUSTINE P. - FOUNDER - MILLION DOLLAR BRANDERS PTY.LTD

HOW TO GET $#IT DONE

Have a Plan

A few years into my advertising career I worked for a large telecommunications corporation. I'd often listen to Jim Rohn, who said, "Work full time on your job and part time on your fortune" If you paused and read that again because you didn't quite get it, this is the chapter for you!

Anyone can blame their job for stopping them from achieving their dreams. It happens quite frequently, actually. It's what leads to those dull, melodramatic excuses that make you feel like someone is dragging a chair across the floor right by you.

You think *I'll do it later*.

Why not now? What's wrong with you that you can't?

If you want to do something, business-wise or even as your golden accomplishment, you've got to have a plan to make it work. If you don't have a plan—a set goal with a tangible list of actions to live your dream —you are not going to be very happy. As they say...

"If you don't build your dream, someone else will hire you to help build theirs."

"Goal" is an overused concept, that is under utilized most of the time. Viewing goals as a way to manifest results for what *you* claim matters to *you,* is very effective. You need to:

- Have a 3, 6, 9, and 12 month plan
- Set your goals really high, because by the time 3 months is up and you start hitting goals, you're ready to begin on your 6-month goals
- Recognize goals as a machine that never stops working—the centrifugal force of your success

Now it's time to evaluate the toughest question: how am I going to do this?

Sometimes it's easiest to find your "how" when you know "why" things aren't working. Take your relationships—is something missing that you can't pinpoint? How about your career; are you drifting like a piece of wood on the ocean, hitting calm waters one day and stormy tides the next?

Goals help connect what is missing with your successes, which positively impact everything. Everything is interlinked.

Before we break down the three areas of goals that you really need to focus on to gain that balance—the links that connect all areas of your life, you need to think about one word that we all kind of like—rewards!

What is a good **reward** for you? It will be dependent on a few things:

- What do you enjoy?
- What is your budget?
- What inspires you to keep achieving, so you can claim more rewards? (Rewards will keep you motivated both short and long term)

Rewards should be dependent on:

- How long it took you to achieve the goal
- How easily it can be enjoyed without creating stress in another area of your life
- How likely it will really be the "!" on your "kicka$$ Achievement" list

For me, there is no reward that doesn't involve exhilaration of some sort for my life. For example, I have made it a firm commitment to be rewarded in these various ways as I achieve the goals I've set out to do. Writing this book is certainly one of them, as I want it to be my legacy for the world. Less stuffiness and propriety, more experience and doing!

This book is the first of many goals on my kicka$$ Achievement list. Some of my other goals include:

- Take my entire family on a 1 month holiday around the world (no expenses spared).
- Know that I can support 3 generations of my family without financial worry.
- Start an orphanage in Africa that teaches creative entrepreneurship and business building.
- Host a global TV show that inspires and teaches people who are in unfortunate situations: How to regain their million dollar mindset and give them the confidence to build their own million dollar brand.
- Have a Million Dollar Branders office in every capital city in the world that hires only the best of the best creative's and talent—enabling them to live their dream life and reach their full uncapped potential.
- See all the wonders of the world—with the people I love.
- Create a Justine Pogroske legacy—and give back enough to the world that people remember my name.

Sure these goals might seem **crazy—to you**, but I sure as hell plan to achieve them. Meanwhile, while I'm working towards it, I am aware that life isn't worth the pot you piss in, if you don't laugh and smile along the way. It's not just work. It's not just fun. It comes down to balance and self-recognition that you're doing a bang-up job, with what you've set out to do.

Some people say rewards shouldn't be attached to money, but I challenge you to think differently. If you are turning your financial fortunes around, why couldn't you budget in a reward that's financially driven?

Everyone looks at and defines "a lot of money" differently. For me, it's the house on the oceanfront. It's the exotic holidays with no time constraints, due to money. It's my white Lamborghini, with red leather interior seats sitting cozily in my four-car garage . It is not having to worry about where the next dollars come from, especially when it comes to health. "A lot of money" means the ability to look after my loved ones and friends to a limitless level.

Additionally, I desire to experience many of the things that my parents have never known, but now I have. I find it hard to find anything that beats working towards achieving my goals and experiencing the rewards of achieving them. This is where you should begin to question what actually drive your success?

So take a second..... a blank piece of paper, write down what you actually want to achieve and why. Knowing your WHY, will get you through the toughest moments that make you want to give up.

PUTTING IT ALL TOGETHER

Do you understand how it all started? Success doesn't come from people just coming together and making a lot of money. There's a massive, Grand Canyon-sized gap in the middle of that. When future successful people first came together they each had:

- A set of strengths to offer
- Determination to stick it out

- The know-how and commitment to make it happen
- Endurance
- Extraordinary belief

There is no such thing as overnight success. It was only after these things were in place that the money came. And more often than not, only after this immense amount of work has been done do others begin to know who you are. Don't seek out people to make you rich; create something that makes it mandatory for you to be noticed. It all comes together...but there is an order to the process.

There is planning.

And likely adjusting.

Always have a plan...

> ***Plans can change because life changes but don't be hard on yourself if something doesn't work out.***

Everyone is different, and they need different things in order to achieve their goals, depending on their strengths and weaknesses. This is where it becomes important to mentally commit to what you have to do. Align yourself with strong people who know how to move in the right direction. These are people who have achieved things in life, they are your support.

Three must-haves in your support department are:

1. **A "Dream Team"**: these are the people that are "unconditional" to you in their love and support. They may not agree with your goals, but they are tried and true fans of you. When you need tough love, they give it. If you need someone just to listen while you rant like a lunatic and diffuse, they do so with an attentive ear. When you are having a rough day, they don't mind motivating you. This may be someone who has already taken big strides on the journey you are in, and they can teach you the little tricks to get you over the biggest obstacles. Anything goes...it's unconditional.

2. **The right success resources**: not having money is not an excuse. Turn away from the dark, never ending pit of excuses and look into the mirror. There's your answer—you and your efforts will guide you to the resources you need. Connect with people who have system's in place and know how to help you enhance your efforts to make them count for more. I can assure you, it's better to work an extra job to afford the right success resources, than it is to dwell in the land of underachievers. I didn't always have money, but the fire and drive people saw within me lead them to guide me, they knew I was a future investment. Be a person, people want to invest in. You may be surprised at how many people love this trait and make time to help you if you just show a little "extra" interest.

3. **Find an online mentor**: we have access to amazing mentors (free online). Find one who you resonate with that has exceptional qualities that will help you achieve your goals.

What I love about a mentor you never meet face-to-face is that they are not afraid to lay it out on the line. You should encourage blunt honesty, followed by a conversation that gets you to the conclusion you need. Don't be a buttercup—be a bold seeker of solutions.

> *Nothing in life is unattainable. Life just wants you to show it how badly you want it.*

There are three main areas in your life that will contribute to your long term success and always throw challenges at you:

1) <u>Health and Wellness</u>
- Personal relationships
- Your discipline for positive results
- Your appearance

2) <u>Career</u>
- Your hunger for learning and growth
- Your strengths and weaknesses
- Your environment

3) <u>Money</u>
- Your money "belief system"
- Money management
- Mentors and resources

With any dream you have in life, the important thing you need to remember is:

When things go wrong, don't think like a loser.

Don't be a loser, be someone who just does. I've already told you, you don't have to be an academic. If you are, this is great. Yay for you, but academics alone don't guarantee success. Working you're a$$ off and working smart will.

Are you ready to stand in the line-of-fire when things go wrong? Sometimes life may slap you across the face and others, it may pat you on the back. It's all well, as it's a starting point. It is all part of your growth and the universe testing you how badly you want it.

STRAIGHT TALK: QUESTIONS FOR HEALTH AND WELLNESS

1. What are your day to day habits?

2. Are you challenging yourself to be the strongest, healthiest version of yourself?

3. What does the future version of yourself look like? (How do you walk, talk, act, speak)

4. Do your personal relationships have balance or are you always throwing a counter-punch just to make things even? And how sick are you of doing this?

5. Who are the people in your life inspire and drive you?

6. When was the last time you did something to become a better person, just because you wanted to and knew it was worth it?

7. Look up into the sky. How's your relationship with that big universe and that one thing you believe is greater than yourself?

8. When you look down at what you're wearing—at this very minute—would you want anyone to see you? What would their first impression of you be based on your outer appearance?

He who endures conquers.

Having your personal life in order—from the inside out—is important because you go everywhere your decisions take you. You can escape some things for a bit of time, but you can never escape that one you know is accountable for what you do. YOU!

STRAIGHT TALK: QUESTIONS FOR YOUR CAREER

1. When was the last time you took charge of a task that was outside of your comfort zone?

2. What is your WHY for wanting to achieve success?

3. Are you surrounded by the people who can help you do great things?

4. Career wise - where do you see your future-self in 1,2,3, 5-10 years time?

5. Is your current job or career path making you happy?

6. You walk into a room on the day of a big meeting, what do people think when they first look at you? Is this what you want them to think?

7. Someone screwed you over big time. What is your response? Do you give them the victory, perhaps ignore them, or just learn your lessons and focus on what's important—you?

8. Who is one powerful business person that you'd like to be for a day, and why? What will it take to be more like them?

9. Do you have your $#IT together to achieve your goals? What's your plan of action? You need to take strategic steps to achieve what you want for success.

10. Look at the five closest friends in your network.

   ◦ Are they successful?
   ◦ Can you learn from them?
   ◦ Will they help you get to where you need to be?

***Don't just be a player.
Be a game changer.***

Other people don't make your success. They can guide and mentor, but if they are worth anything at all they will not devote their time to someone who doesn't invest their time into their own results. And why should they? If you don't show you care by taking tangible actions with your goals, they have zero—zilch—reasons to engage with you. If that doesn't jump start you to thinking more strategically, remember that there is someone else catching up to you right now, that will do what it takes. Don't get mad at them when they pass you by and make $#it happen.

STRAIGHT TALK: MONEY QUESTIONS

1. What are your goals and priorities?

2. What does your future self look like? (How are you dressed, what house do you live in, what car do you drive?)

3. Are you living like royalty while making a pauper's salary?

4. Do you know what the smartest investments for your career return are at this current moment? And, do you invest in these things?

5. How do you reach your most important financial decisions you must make?

6. Are you investing or saving in the right places? For the right things?

7. What steps do you take to ensure your financial clout goes up, instead of remaining stagnant?

8. Do you have a "dream board" with the things you would do if you had the financial means to do them?

9. Financial well-being can mean something different to every person.

   ○ What does it mean to you?
   ○ How do you plan for your long-term financial future?
   ○ What efforts are most important to your legacy?

> ***"Money is a result, wealth is a result, health is a result, illness is a result, your weight is a result. We live in a world of cause and effect."***
> **–T. Harv Eker**

We can work and save hard to make our goals become a reality, and this is great, of course. It's the start of big things. The other end of this equation is always saying you'll start saving, investing, and managing your monies better next...week, month, year, etc. We cannot be truly free individuals if we don't have financial freedom. Why wait until you are at the breaking point to do what you've wanted to do all along?

Do you really want to be the last one out of the starting gate for success? Hell no, you don't!

MAKE $#IT HAPPEN CHECKLIST

✔ **Write a list of goals and put them everywhere**: These reminders will serve you well and you will begin to manifest your goals.

✔ **Write down your dream team**: The list doesn't have to be large, just effective.

✔ **Create exhilarating rewards**: What's going to get you so excited and feed your adrenaline and drive?

✔ **Don't throw up a flag at every wild idea**: Sometimes the wildest ideas are the best. Need an example? The internet. Need another? Email.

✔ **Work out your reason and your why for achieving success**: By knowing the factors that can be our driving force we can keep on going even when we're having a day from hell.

"GREAT SPIRITS
ARE OFTEN
CHALLENGED
BY MEDIOCRE
MINDS.
STAY TRUE
TO YOURSELF."

Justine P.

JUSTINE P. - FOUNDER - MILLION DOLLAR BRANDERS PTY LTD

WORK SMART, NOT HARD
Have a Damn Good Plan

I'll admit it right away—I'm still learning about the importance of having a plan. Throughout my life, and probably yours, I've heard everyone say, "you need a plan." Do this. Do that. It's logical, I suppose, but there is a big problem that comes with just tossing a plan out there, and that is:

BIG plans mean nothing without BIG actions.

It's more like flipping the pinky. You need to show that you've got the basics down of your business. A complex business plan doesn't necessarily do that. Where in the history of success does it state that a forty-page plan is the only option you have? Assuredly, two pages of quality content are better than forty pages of babble. You've got to work smart.

You need an understanding of what you're building...

- Yourself
- Your relationship with your brand and a business that is reflective of your hard work and entrepreunial effort.

Be flexible and adaptable to your changing needs. Look at your plan as your computer's hard drive—it has all the details of how your system is going to work. Business can be a real bastard at times, just like a broken internet connection. Things fall apart. When you have faster internet speed, things go great, but when it slows down, everything seems to short circuit. And if there's a malfunction, you're rendered useless. Being pliable to the necessary adjustments becomes critical in these situations.

It's easier to make shifts and adjustments if you know that you are gaining insight and wisdom from those who have already worked a plan.

The best planning involves creating the best partnerships.

Surround yourself with resources that help it all come together. You might be at a time when you have to hand off the project to someone else who is better suited. Your business plan should highlight your brand, and when it's put together right, it's easily relayed. It speaks to all areas of your business.

THE DETAILS ARE IN THE PLAN(NING)

Every business is different, however there is a basic formula and skeleton for success from what I have learnt. The key elements that have contributed to the success of Million Dollar Branders have included:

- **Our Summary and Story**
  - Background
  - Vision
  - Mission Statement
- **Our Environment**
  - Company culture (Our dream team's mindset, attitude and work ethic)
  - Your company alignments and thought leadership skills
- **Our Kick Ass Goals**
  - Objectives
  - Tactics
  - Future Expansions & Exit Plan
- **Our Million Dollar Hit List of Customers**
  - Ideal Customer
  - Non-ideal Customer
- **Our Competitors**
  - Competitor SWOT Analysis
    (strengths, weaknesses, opportunities, threats)
  - Bold Competitive Marketing Strategies
- **Our Services**
  - Current Services &Products
  - Future Services & Products
- **Promotions & Strategies**
  - Online Marketing

- Social Media Marketing
- Content Marketing
- Email Marketing
- SEO & Link building
- Website Advertising
- Video Marketing
- Viral Campaigns
- Influencers /Partnerships
    - **Offline Marketing**
        - Direct Marketing & Print
        - Public & Press Relations
- **Financial**
    - Expected Monthly Expenses
    - Expected Monthly Income
    - Expected Marketing Budget
    - Expected Re-investment & EXIT plan
- **Measurement**
    - Brand Awareness
    - Website Traffic and Conversions
    - Social Media
    - Email "Gold List"
    - Video and multimedia

Visit **www.milliondollarbranders.com/mshbp** and print off your complimentary game changer **MAKE $#IT HAPPEN** business plan template. More detailed explanations for each area are included to help you make the most out of your business plan.

DELEGATING

If you're a control freak, you probably despise the word delegate. Get over it! I get your resistance... You want to hold on to every single little thing when it's your baby. It's personal, and the perspective gets muddled in your big ego. No one can do what you're doing as well as you.

Be real! No matter how much you love your business, there are other people better suited to perform some tasks. There are some things you are a master of, but some things you are not, so get over your effin' self.

> ***If you are afraid to hand over work to others, you have not hired the right people.***

The biggest challenge I've seen people face is that they are logical operators trying to keep up in the fast lane of creative efforts. They don't understand investments in creativity, just as creative people often are at risk of not understanding the importance of the logical steps. This is why you need resources that are the best of the best—better than you in the areas where you risk failure without said resources. And you must do your due diligence so you can trust them and delegate what you don't do well.

> ***Plan to invest big now, knowing it will pay off later***

I'll never forget an advertising challenge that my company, Million Dollar Branders took on. The guy came to me after hearing me speak at one of my keynote events. His business had some challenges, and his product looked like crap. Although he approached me, when we first sat down he was majorly reluctant due to his past history with other marketing thugs. I had a big vision for his brand. This was tough for his logical mind to process. He thought he had a good foundation but his product revealed a different truth, as his sales were not converting the way they should have been. I explained that people are buying "an experience," not just a product.

There are times when you play the game, and there are times when you call the bluff. I finally told him that it was his choice to make. He could invest now and trust me to take his brand to the next level, or he could skimp now and try investing in other things, but the chances were that he'd be going to market and people wouldn't even look at what he had to offer. He disliked what I said, but got the point.

What we need to hear isn't always pretty, and sugar-coating sure as hell isn't effective.

When building your brand ask yourself:

- What are you giving your clients or customers that is different from your competition?
- Take away your signature item. What else sells your brand and makes you unique?

This is how you begin working smart, not hard.

Know who you are, and who you are not. If you're not creative, don't try to be. Outsource it. What is the point of working until 4 AM with online tutorials about creativity, that neither motivate nor inspire you enough to fully get it? Never do things you hate, it sucks the joy right out of the day, really.

I know what I hate a lot—cleaning my house. I'm not good at it because I'm thinking about how much it sucks. When I try to do it, it takes me twice as long because of this. Paying the expert that can clean my house the right way makes all the sense in the world. Honestly, I'd rather find an extra ten hours of work a week than to clean my house. The same mindset applies to business. Why spend ten hours on what really doesn't light you up or move you forward. Put it in an expert's hands.

SPEAK THE LANGUAGE OF OTHERS TO ATTRACT THEM

You always need to have your hustle going and bring your "A-game." A bad day is no excuse and giving up when things go to $#IT isn't either. So what if you have a crap job or whatever—if you keep harping on about it, it won't help get you out of the job, you will only feel more stuck. Your situation will not be permanent if you begin to recognize the power and influence you have just through the way you talk with others.

If the people you're around are complaint enablers, change your language and find the doers.

Negative people get exactly what they ask for. So, watch your words, what you speak you attract. Lou Holtz said it well: *"Don't tell people about your problems. 90% of them don't care and the other 10% are glad you got them."*

You have to be aware of your communication and actions at all times. You could be sitting next to a billionaire who may lead you to the next opportunity or adventure. They could see a skill set in you or like the way you act: your charisma, your actions, etc. When they connect those qualities with attraction-based language, you are a step closer to making $#IT happen.

Your Attitude = Your Altitude

Those who have proven success don't need you nearly as much as you need them. No-one owes you anything.

Attitude is everything. You have to work hard and do so positively. If you come across as a struggling new business, no one is going to take you seriously. If you don't believe you're capable of taking on a big opportunity that comes your way, others won't believe you deserve it. In the words of Tom Bilyeu "You need to take action and act as if". Be the person you want to be tomorrow.

Set yourself high goals and standards - Stick to them at whatever cost.

DIVIDE YOUR TIME

As the Director of my company, it's very easy for me to be distracted when I get to work. I walk in, and if I allow it, a million people can pull me in a million different directions. This feeling of being stretched too thin is familiar to dedicated entrepreneurs, too.

When you are making $#IT happen people will come up to you all day long and ask you questions, want a bit of your time. "I have this cool idea" they'll say. "Can you help me with this? It'll just take a little bit of your time," they beg. Add up all that time at the end of the month and OMG—that's your time that you gave away and it made you no money, and you can never—never—get it back!

You need to have discipline and think about what you are going to do to make money. Making money is what it all comes down to at the end of the day when you're building a business and building your brand.

Ask yourself one question whenever you are in doubt:

> *Is this going to make me money?*
> *If the answer is no, it goes to the*
> *bottom of the list.*

What never goes to the bottom of the list? There are three things:

1. **Water and Food**: Drink and eat the right things that give you the energy to take care of business . Your results are directly linked to how you fuel your body. Your body will thank you.

2. **Exercising**: Movement and exercise helps to clear the mind and keeps you at the top of your game.

3. **Family time**: Family time is valuable, they won't be around forever. Don't have regrets that you didn't spend enough time with them, when there was time to give.

4. **Friends**: Value those who value you. It's that simple.

These 4 things can have a domino effect on your life. Without making sure you are disciplined in these areas, you reduce your chances of achieving success. It's that simple...... Balance is the key, and it begins with you.

> ## *Be aware of what you give away, and to whom.*

Working smart means, working towards what is productive and good within every area of your life. Success is purposeful and forward moving; spinning your wheel's like a moron and hoping to get somewhere is not.

MAKE $#IT HAPPEN CHECKLIST

✔ **Make your to-do list the night before and prepare for your business the next day**: Whether it's marketing, advertising, reading an article, attending an event, etc.

✔ **Remember time is currency**: You have 1,440 minutes in a day. Make each one count. Imagine each minute has a dollar value. Why give priority to what doesn't help you in some manner?

✔ **Perfect the skill of saying no**: You can do this without being rude. When you say no, use charisma and etiquette.

✔ **With your business plans make sure you have purposeful, measurable tasks noted**: Remember to download the detailed version of the MAKE $#IT HAPPEN business plan template.

✔ **Make yourself a priority**: Nothing else is going to work out to its fullest potential, if you don't make yourself a priority. Put YOU first.

"WORK WILE THEY SLEEP. LEARN WHILE THEY PARTY. SAVE WHILE THEY SPEND. LIVE LIKE THEY DREAM, AND MAKE YOUR MILLIONS QUIETLY."

Justine P.

JUSTINE P. - FOUNDER - MILLION DOLLAR BRANDERS PTY.LTD

IDEAS ARE CURRENCY
Execution is Essential

All people who have made it BIG, have one thing in common: they understand that ideas without execution are $#IT. An idea is never enough. Let's face it if you have that million-dollar idea, but you don't do anything with it, the idea will fall off the face of the earth. Or, someone else will have the same idea and take action where you did not. Then you risk becoming one of those pathetic souls who brag's about having thought about an idea long ago, adding "if only" to the end. (E.g. "If only I executed my UBER idea before UBER, I would have made millions"). How annoying..... Please don't be that person—ever.

The crazy, 'effin fantastic thing about ideas is that they can range from the practical to the obscure.

If you think you have to be a rocket scientist to come up with an idea that people will go wild over, think again. Consider these examples...

Combine a rock and a pet, and what do you get? The Pet Rock. This idea is the brainchild of Gary Dahl, and it earned him a massive $15,000,000 in just six months. How many doubters do you think Gary ran into when he first presented that idea?

When you mix a yellow circle and a happy, smiling face telling you to "have a nice day" what do you get? You get $500,000,000 million in sales. This is what two brothers, Bernard and Murray Spain, did in the early 1970s. You want to know what's really painful? They were the ones that saw its potential, the man who actually created it—and did not trademark it—made a mere $45 on that smiley face. Love or loathe that yellow smiley face...you definitely know it.

Combine a love for the ridiculous and a blanket with sleeves, and what do you get? The Snuggie, which is Scott Boilen of All star Products $200,000.000 idea. Outrageous marketing that draws attention can work with the right product. The Snuggie is almost like a cult classic of gifts—and even an accessory for Snuggie Pub crawls in some places! So, for those of you who snubbed the Snuggie...I bet you wouldn't snub the profits it garnered.

Are you catching on yet? Don't discredit ideas and put them aside just because someone doesn't "get it" or likes what you've thought of. That one person isn't the world of marketing or the world of buyers. Are they even a target buyer? You've got to use some common sense and due diligence to tap into what people really want...it's sometimes quite surprising.

CURRENCY IS ALWAYS MOVING

I had an electrician come to me, and he said he wanted to be different to anyone in his market. He'd seen what I could do, loved my stuff, and wanted me to help him create distinction by coming up with a brand for his business.

The best way to start with this type of request is a tag line, and we came up with : At Pulse Electrical - *'We turn you on.'*

Simple, precise, and a delicious innuendo tangled in between. Today, this tag line is out there on everything associated with this business. When I'm sitting in traffic and look over to see one of their vehicles, I always smile because I know the impact the tag line has had on the company, especially when people read it, point and laugh. Who forgets a tag line like that? Not many.

Branding is your currency, and you can make anything sexy, sleek, and interesting with the right approach. Yes, he is a skilled electrician, that is highly talented, but ultimately, people are buying his brand.

IDEA STRATEGIES

The number one thing that you must do with your idea, is not be protective of it. If you don't share and engage others with what your concept is, you are not working smart. What if you are wasting a lot of time and effort on nothing?

Share your ideas with people who are smarter than you and know how to analyze them from various angles and perspectives.

Engage those who are smarter than you in certain areas and allow them to expose what's good about your ideas, and what is perhaps flawed (Engage your dream team). These are the people who will keep it real with you and don't blow smoke up your butt, just to appease your bad idea (if it's truly bad).

I had an investor I worked with once that refused to sign non-disclosure agreements (NDA's). His reason for it was sound. He said that with intellectual property someone could be working on that same idea anywhere else in the world. There was a chance they could do it better and have a sounder team executing it. A race to the finish to be the one who got their first, was not what this guy was interested in. He believed in good execution, and so do I.

If someone has the same idea as you but executes it faster and better, you only have yourself to blame.

While most people believe that you invest in branding and image after your idea has proven itself, this is completely wrong. I'd dare say it is just as wrong as putting a pickle in a glass of red wine. If you believe that marketing and branding come after everyone loves your idea, you're wrong. They are intricately linked to what sells your idea. Getting an idea to take off requires intensive and constant energy and effort. You must give it your all, and if you don't believe in it enough to do so, or you should not do it at all. Investing in the minimal things such as a logo or an effective business card are not options. If you choose not to do it properly the first time, good luck with getting anyone to believe you actually have a million-dollar idea.

It is ALL in the execution. First, it's how your product looks when it goes to market. And after you succeed, the next challenge is maintaining the stature, once you have a fantastic brand or platform.

After some initial work with a one-time client I had them say to me, *"Great, so you have created the brand. It's awesome and doing great in the market! So, I now I can hire a cheaper graphic designer to slap on a logo onto some images, and that's it!"* I looked at her and shook my head. Whether she realized it or not, she had totally devalued the work we had been building toward— and missed the greater vision. When maintaining a strong brand consistency is key.

> *A professional brander looks at the long-term value and life of the brand and product. We do an "ideation forecast". We make sure the brand's execution stays strong throughout it's life cycle.*

You see, execution is something that is constantly moving and in motion. It's an ongoing process. A strong brand involves maintaining, monitoring, and adjusting. You want to remain relevant once you've reached a million-dollar level. You want to stand out in a sea of other brand's. It requires hard work and endless effort. In the words of Don Draper from Madmen *"the second you sign a client is the second you lose them"*. Additionally, when a business starts, there is always a peak and always a drop. A good business owner will recognize this and never drop the ball on the ongoing execution of the brand. They do whatever it takes, whenever it is needed. They invest, because they see the value in creating a legacy.

MAKE $#IT HAPPEN CHECKLIST

✔ **Don't determine your own fate before you give it a try**: If you don't have the ability to look at a rock as a source of making millions, don't assume it can't be done. Ask an expert if it has "legs".

✔ **Be willing to dedicate yourself to the intensive work**: Building a brand and business really is blood, sweat, and tears that you willingly sacrifice. You must research your ideas and be fearless in working with people smarter than you.

✔ **Don't be stingy with your concepts**: If you are not going to share your ideas and concepts with anyone, they will fall off the face of the earth, spiraling down somewhere into the abyss.

✔ **Execute on your ideas**: Take action over daydreaming.

✔ **Commit to what it takes make your idea work**: Success doesn't come easy. If you give up on the first bump in the road, or even the second or third, you're going to fail. Do you really want that?

"ALWAYS BRING YOUR A-GAME. PEOPLE ARE BUYING YOU."

Justine P.

JUSTINE P. - FOUNDER - MILLION DOLLAR BRANDERS PTY LTD

GET OUT OF YOUR BOX

Don't Stifle Yourself

Many business owners risk not thinking outside the box, or they stop once they've reached a certain level of success. There is no reason to stop wanting to stand out and excel in your business—you can never make yourself too successful.

Stepping outside the box and doing something that is noticed is a sign of strength. You get more people to take note of you. You know what I say to that? "That's so damn amazing!"

In a world where there are so many mainstream businesses, how do you stand out?

Very few businesses are one-of-a-kind, which means you have to learn to create distinction for yourself. My company and I have always been on a mission to help businesses invest in the right steps to be remembered. Branding is an essential part of this process, and much of this work is done up-front. You want to go out into the world with a bang, not feeling like a dud.

I had a client, a rubbish removal company that thought they couldn't look sexy because of what they did. This is what I told them: '*we are going to address the stigma of what you do.*' People are judgmental, yes. What people don't realize is that rubbish removal workers can make really great salaries, don't have to work as long of hours as many people, and they are smart. If that's not impressive enough, they also get holidays and weekends off, typically. Those are job perks many people strive to earn.

We ended up repositioning their brand to get rid of the stigma. The advert we put together to do this was memorable. The workers pull up in front of a job site and walk out of the van putting a peppermint in their mouth, wearing tuxedoes with roses on their lapels, and white gloves. Then they knock on the door, "Hi, It's Rubbish Brothers. We're here to collect your rubbish."

This is an example of positioning and making a dynamic impression.

If you can't turn yourself into that outside the box organization, pay someone who will.

This transformation isn't brain surgery. It involves research and tapping into a new vein that can highlight your business in a way that's favorable to your end goals. It may not be visually beautiful—advertising eye candy—but the result of being effective is what counts. This is the type of work that ad agencies do—they show you how outside the box thinking pays rewards. As creatives, we get paid the big bucks for this because it is an art and psychology. It is a master skill to connect people with services and products in a clever and engaging way. At Million Dollar Branders it has been my aim to teach clients how to zig when other people zag.

If you assess your competition and they are all doing flyers, you do not want to do a flyer. It will do nothing for you. You're playing on the same level as everyone else, and it's incredibly drab. Go a different direction. And, please, stay away from clichés, because they are horrible. Truly, they are. When people zig, you need to zag.

THE STATS DON'T LIE

Jeff Bezos, CEO of Amazon is credited for saying, "Your brand is what other people say about you when you're not in the room." When people talk, the $#IT spreads much faster than the good. This is why every action matters for branding. If your business is in its infancy, brand before it grows any further. If your business is at the edge of a plateau or has never taken off, look to branding.

These numbers reveal the big picture[3]:

- **78%** of consumers feel that when a company is focused on content, they are more trustworthy.

- Businesses with blogs generate an average of **67%** more leads per month.

- Over the past 3 years, a person checking their email on their mobile device has increased by **180%**.

- An estimated **70%-80%** of consumers ignore ads on the sides of websites and search results. They are deemed less trustworthy.

- The right color can improve readership by **40%**, as well as be more visually appealing.

- Images are processed about **60,000 times faster** than words. This is why the proper visual in a logo is important.

- Recognition equals value. Instagram has about **40 million images** posted on it a day. Over **10,000** of them include the Starbucks logo—either intentionally or unintentionally.

- If your brand has a signature color, it can increase its recognition by **80%**.

- **90%** of purchases are decided subconsciously, which makes emotions a huge part of all branding.

- In **10 seconds,** a consumer forms the first impression of a brand's logo. However, it takes **5-7 impressions** for consumers to recognize it.

- **91%** of consumers are more likely to buy from what they feel is an authentic brand; however, if you don't know your target audience you'll be in trouble. Peoples' perceptions of honesty and authenticity change between generations.

- Consumers love social media, which is why **71%** will purchase from brands that have a presence on it. This means that you have to ensure your URLs are chosen wisely and easily traced to your business.

- First impressions are critical for developing brand loyalty. **48%** of consumers become loyal to the brand they purchase or experience first.

- **82%** of investors believe brand strength and name recognition are important in guiding them to investment decisions (per Reuters).

To think that you can go against the grain and defy all these telling statistics, is setting yourself up for poor results. You can't be lazy about vigorously ensuring that your branding is in order. Would you rather grow one business successfully or keep starting over with new lessons learned, and a potentially great idea wasted?

TAKE THE BRANDING CHALLENGE

You're thinking of your brand and what you wish it to be. Look at what your competitors are currently doing. Now ask: Do you want to copy them or accelerate past them?

Here's a little test to see if you're memorable, or even have a brand?

> If your life was at stake and someone was about to shoot you or your competitor, depending on brand, who would they shoot first?

If you cannot immediately say, *not me*, it's time to start evaluating. Here are some questions about your brand that can help to guide you:

- Is your product one that has a market?
- What strategies were used to create your branding plan?
- Do you know who your target client is?
- After a consumer views your current digital presence, are they compelled to purchase?
- How does your product stand out from your competitors?
- If you had to explain your product or service in three to five seconds, could you?

Your brand is an extension of you.

If it is just good, decent, or okay—do not put it to market. Take the time to make it exceptional, a show-stopper in every single way. This is the art of building a million dollar brand and empire.

Be a hallmark amongst the competition. Give your competition something to worry about! Be a benchmark for them. Do it properly the first time. You only get one chance to take it to market. A million dollar brand is born when it changes conventions and inspires.

Be that inspiration. Create a legacy through brilliant brand presence. In a fast moving world there is only room for the best of the best.

MAKE $#IT HAPPEN CHECKLIST

✔ **Successful brands cannot be found inside the box**: If you want to create distinction, you'll have to venture outside the box.

✔ **It doesn't matter if your product is the best thing since sliced bread**: If people don't connect with it, they are not going to buy it.

✔ **Your competition should be looking up to you**: More than you are chasing after them.

✔ **If your first impression shows a lack of effort more than an investment in strategy**: You just lost a large number of potential clients or customers.

✔ **Be confident**: You've got to invest in yourself and show you're worth it.

"WHEN YOU ARE INSPIRING OTHERS YOU ARE WINNING."

Justine P.

JUSTINE P. - FOUNDER - MILLION DOLLAR BRANDERS PTY LTD

SAY LITTLE; DO LOTS
Create Maximum Impact

In advertising, it is all about creating maximum impact in a few words. People do not have the attention span for more. If you're an entrepreneur or business owner you need to understand this. You are vulnerable to over complicating stuff—a lot—and much of the time this is because you are too close to the product.

Stand back and gain some perspective.

One of the largest challenges with clients is helping them to gain perspective. I've met people who were so married to their product that they thought any idea that wasn't generated by them, was useless and uninformed. Yet, they were hiring me as an expert to help them brand their product.

Think about this...if they had the formula in place, they could just pay a staff member to implement it. Case closed. Why, exactly, would Million Dollar Branders be necessary? We are only of value to those who will allow us to delve into and extract the key elements that will brand their product successfully. It isn't always going to be blinking and shining. At times, subtlety is necessary depending on your product or idea. Either way, you are making a strategic decision to go big and bold when you market your distinctive brand properly. You have so few seconds, 3-5 at most. People don't have large attention spans. A perfect example is an airport billboard. The message has to be captured in the fraction of time that it takes a car to pass it by.

Perhaps the toughest challenge you'll face is realizing that you don't market to your tastes, but to your target clients' tastes. Believe it or not, they may be very different. Remember this! Take yourself out of your head, and put yourself in the head of your client.

Don't sell a product that YOU want to buy. Sell a product your CLIENTS want to buy.

It's not about your experience; it's about your client's experience. When leading global keynote speakers present on stage, they make it all about their audience, not themselves. It's a proposition to your audience, not to your ego. These types of skills carry over into all areas of life. Even a good date falls into this way of presenting. In my younger days, I experienced this scenario first-hand on a date, like so many men and women have.

There I was with this guy that was completely arrogant and full of himself. Talk, talk, talk. I texted my best friend and asked for some advice on what I should do. Her reply: you can make it the best date ever. Just let him talk about himself all night. So, I did, and finally,

I made it through to the end—that point where I could go my way, and he could go his. And God willing, the two of us would never cross paths again.

The next day, I got a text from this guy. He told me that he'd just had the best date he'd ever had. I'm thinking, *are you kidding me, this guy's a selfish a$$hole* (and I laughed)... but I'll tell you what, it did teach me how to conduct successful business.

The first thing I do when I walk into a room is ask how I can serve.

If you make it all about your clients, it's a successful path for you. It's not about you and your vision. Creating the best brand involves driving someone else's vision and passion so that they look at your product and think, *"I have to have it"*. They may not know why, exactly, but something is telling them they must.

Apple is a great example of this. Did you know this[4]? As of April 2016, there were one billion "active" Apple devices—one device for every seven people in this world. Does everyone logically need these devices? Probably not; however, the connection to them is emotional and appealing on a highly personal level, which is an indicator of a very powerful brand. A company like Apple can survive the bumps and bruises of a poorly executed launch or marketing strategy. Can your business or idea do the same?

THE BIGGEST MISTAKE

A lot of people make the mistake of doing a website or brochure and cramming every thought they've had for the last decade into them. This is a costly mistake because people will not pay attention. It's overkill and distracting. It's garbage.

Think of those days when you have so much going on that your head is clogged up with ideas, over stimulation, and information. Do you grow more engaged as a result? Highly unlikely, if you're being honest. You shut down and are less functional and interested.

Imagine, your muddled mind is your website for your product. Someone comes to look at it, and they shut down instead of open up. You must do everything possible to ensure that you are inviting them into not just a website, but an experience. This will limit your bounce rate.

Think back to Apple for a second. Three words that describe their marketing and branding are crisp, clear, and uncluttered. This lends to the experience and what may seem like it's "cold" is actually inviting. On average, you have fifteen seconds to capture someone's attention. Knowing the formula to make those seconds count is critical, and assuredly, taking the "less is more" approach does help.

TWO GUIDELINES

You don't need ten billion pictures on your advert to describe what you're doing. A line of copy on a white sheet of paper can be all you need. A clever tag line or video can be worth more than five pages of text. Your goal is to precisely share what you want your client to know.

You can do this by following these three guidelines:

1. Create an experience.
2. Cut out all the crap to get you the results you want.
3. If you go digital, remember you still need to add a human element.

There is a rising trend that's refreshing right now. People are growing sicker of people who talk crap. They now want to hear how it is. "Give it to me straight." This is because we don't have the time to waste.

> *We'll take a pass before we spend time reading paragraphs and paragraphs of copy or watching a five-minute ad. People just grab their phones when this happens, they're not interested.*

When you're creating your brand, ask: is this going to be engaging? Not to me, but to my audience. Will they get the idea and concept?

Hint: Your brand also needs to also match your advertising medium. For example if you are a funeral parlor you are not going to put a full page print add in GQ magazine. A good experts will advise you of your "fit" in the market from the moment you sit down in your initial consultation.

ATTENTION!

Humans do not have a great attention span any longer. According to scientists[5], "The age of smart phones has left humans with such a short attention span even a goldfish can hold a thought for longer."Goldfish can hold on for 9 seconds, whereas humans average 6-8 seconds.

The statistics support the "less is more" model[6]:

The average attention span in 2015	8.25 seconds
The average attention span in 2000	12 seconds
The average attention span of a goldfish	9 seconds
Percent of teens who forget major details of close friends and relatives	25 %
Percent of people who forget their own birthdays from time to time	7 %
Average number of times per hour an office worker checks their email inbox	30
Average length watched of a single internet video	2.7 minutes

There are additional statistics that relate to internet browsing and attention span in specific, which include[7]:

Percent of page views that last **less** than 4 seconds	17 %
Percent of page views that lasted **more** than 10 minutes	4 %
Percent of words read on web pages with 111 words or less	49 %
Percent of words read on an average (593 words) web page	28 %
Users spend only 4.4 seconds more for each additional 100 words	

These numbers reveal good insight. If you're the one trying to get too much into your content, stop and rethink it. If you *must* do so, do a video. A video can be useful, so long as you make it interesting enough that people want to watch it.

MAKE $#IT HAPPEN CHECKLIST

✔ **It's not about marketing what you want to see or have or do**: You have to market to what your clients wish for and are willing to purchase.

✔ **Remember the world's short attention span**: With ever-increasing short attention spans you have to get your message out there quickly and precisely.

✔ **Be mindful of why your best interest can often be a detached one**: If you're too attached to your product to have any perspective, get a separation and bring in an outside expert from someone who knows their stuff.

✔ **Work with a diverse, proven group of people**: You do not want to only work with people who give you what you want; make sure they are delivering you what you need.

✔ **Say "no" to information dumping**: Do not shove obnoxious amounts of information at consumers, because they will not take the time to try and process your jumbled, pitchy mess.

"MEDIOCRE ATTITUDE LEADS TO MEDIOCRE INCOME.

ONLY YOU DEFINE YOUR WORTH."

Justine P.

JUSTINE P. - FOUNDER - MILLION DOLLAR BRANDERS (PTY LTD)

SMART MONEY

Use Dollars Where They Matter Most

Invest where it counts. If you have a product that needs an online presence or as I call it an online "visual shop front", you need to invest the right amount of money to deliver a website that gives visitors a memorable experience. It should turn them into paying customers and raving fans. By investing in a strong visual shopfront, your business will stand out from your competitors.

The return is as important as the cost.

Get your $#IT done right the first time. Second chances are a pipe dream. If you get one, I guarantee that it'll cost you more than doing it right the first time. Undoing damage that's been done to build your business back up, is a mind-numbing and tedious experience.

A PARABLE OF THE BARGAIN BRANDER

A gentleman creates an appointment with a highly referred branding expert and digital marketer. He states how highly impressed he is with their work, and that he's seen how effective they are.

The two sit down and begin to discuss his needs. "Your work is clever and articulate. That's what I want," he says. "But...it comes down to price."

"What's your budget?" the expert asks.

"I got quoted $900 from another competitor I found online. It covered the website and branding. That's the range I'm willing to pay."

The expert is now left with a choice. Devalue their brand to make a deal with the brand expert or commit to their value and expertise.

The expert doesn't hesitate and replies: *"You should go with that person. I am different, when you engage me, you buy my ideas and articulation. My art. My passion, my mind. I structure your business, position your brand in a fast moving world. I get it noticed."*

The potential client looks at him and nods his head. The branding expert explains:

"I don't just slap things on a page and put something together quickly and say, 'See you later. It's the execution and ideation that is the hardest part. I humanize your brand. I build an emotional attachment between it and the consumer. I create raving fans through psychology and perception. An empire is not built in a day, but once it is built it lasts for a lifetime. I don't build one-hit wonders I build legacies."

This story is an example of what most businesses get when they deal with bargain branders. They seek out those that will give them what they want to hear, rather than what they need to hear. A true branding expert will actually care about you and your brand and will go above and beyond to help you grow.

This is the only way you can become a million-dollar brand.

It's a lesson as old as time: you get what you pay for.

Regardless of the size of business you're envisioning, or even if you're a one-man shop, anyone who will really help you with branding seldom gives you what you say you want. It may even be completely wrong. Professionals always take the time to learn what you need and explain exactly why, as well.

BRANDING IS YOUR FIRST INVESTMENT

Your brand is your essence. It's the problem solving medicine that you give people. It enables people to understand your service offering. It should show them that you will solve their problem.

Subconsciously, everything we do with branding solves a problem. This is true whether you're a presenter, realtor, doctor, or carpet cleaner. You solve a problem for a price and create an experience that is favorable. Your brand should be able to explain what you do immediately. Think of your logo as your "visual elevator pitch."

You must be able to represent your future vision of your company effortlessly. Make it look like you have been around for a long time and have stability so that your clients know they are in good hands.

A good brand doesn't just look pretty, it also has a well-thought out, articulated voice represented through quality copywriting.

So...how do you build an impactful brand?

Make sure your brand:
- Leaves a lasting impact
- Is an experience
- Becomes an addiction amongst consumers

People always want to buy a great campaign. Take a look at Cola-Cola, a brand that has been around since 1886. Many people even know the campaign slogans from its earliest days, because of how effective they were.

The need is simple. People buy you to fix a problem.

Your brand needs to answer and solve the problem in the first second of someone learning who you are. If you have a business card—which you'd best have—the second someone looks at your card, they should be able to get what you do. If they wonder what the point is, or what you're about, you've already lost.

Newsflash: They've checked out and moved on.

Say you're a chiropractor and you hand over a card. When someone looks at it, they should see your logo and get it. *Aha!* They just happen to be suffering a terrible case of "text neck", and there you are. Problem solved. Client gained.

Your brand should answer the basic journalism questions. Who are you? What do you do? How does it work? Why do you do it? Where can I find you?

You need to know your business inside out and be able to articulate it well. Remember those seven billion people in this world? Who are you marketing to and how can you tap into what they need to solve their problems? What makes you the best? Things like *"Because, I'm good at what I do"* just won't cut it in a consumer-saturated market.

These are the tough questions and challenges that branding answers.

ELEMENTS OF A WEBSITE

Your website should be a stand-out online visual shopfront that captures your brand essence in the first 5 seconds. It should focus on making your brand memorable in the vast sea known as the internet. Online, it's much easier to be swept away than remembered.

To be memorable, your website should:

- Be cohesive with your brand
- Have clever, concise copywriting
- Deliver your message in five seconds or less
- Deliver a memorable and interesting experience
- Capture peoples' attention, keep it once you have captured it.

If you put together something that looks like crap, guess what? You'll attract crap and lots of it. Time wasters. Money wasters. Complainers. I don't put my name to anything that isn't clever or immaculate because it has to be reflective of my personality. My standards are high, and I only give the best of the best in the projects Million Dollar Branders takes on.

You've got to be ruthless and a perfectionist. If you're not, find someone else who is, get your brand where you need to be.

Whether your website highlights you, the individual, or your business, you need to make sure it is compelling to those who view it. They're only going to give you a few seconds of their time. Ultimately, you need to connect with them right away, or they will move on.

BUSINESS CARDS ETIQUETTE

Your business card is your personal resume. It draws people in and helps you get the clients you want. It's a reflection of you and your work.

There is also an art to how you should hand out your business cards to potential clients in different cultures. If you're going to a different culture for your growth efforts, do your research before your big meeting.

Million Dollar Branders did some business in Hong Kong, and it was a wonderful trip, and experience. Because I don't work on assumptions, I did the research on cultural business etiquette before the trip which included:

- In Asian culture, business cards are exchanged with two hands as a sign of respect. You are meant to receive it like a gift. It is. That person is giving you an opening into their networking world.

- The business card represents the person to whom you are being introduced, so it is polite to study the card for a while and then put it infront of you on a table or in a business card case.

Consider that every culture has a different way of doing things. Understand that these things could make the difference in your big business deal. For example, if you're conducting business in Japan it's also good to know that packaging is an integral part of the product experience. It is not just about "what holds the product."

Because of this, shoppers place great value in packaging, as well as high expectations about what is contained within it. Their products have a pleasant touch that leads to whatever emotional response it is meant to extract.

You can be the best of the best, but people buy experiences.

It's a cruel world, and people will judge you right away, which is why you must have pride in what you do. If you don't relay that, it's your own damn fault. Keep your head in the game and stay aware that the person who will take you into the million-dollar club may be just around the corner. And they don't necessarily look like a millionaire, either, so remember this.

If you have big goals of becoming a multimillionaire but don't act like one or present yourself as one, your will fail. You need to focus on a great many things, including your image when you are handing out your card.

- **Dress like a million dollars:** Leave the house knowing that you could be signing that next million-dollar deal.

- **Know how to access your business card without looking like a fumbling fool:** Keep it in a business card case or your wallet. Make sure when you pull it out, it looks crisp and neat. Remember, it is a reflection of you and your company. If you pull out a business card that has coffee stains or lipstick marks on it and is dirty, don't be surprised if it doesn't get you that deal you want.

- **Be Articulate:** Educate yourself consistently on current news, affairs, read the latest novels or online e-books. It enables you to have conversation starters for new clients and connect with them on **ANY** level when needed.

Its always judgment day. I know that people are always looking as a thought-leader. When I speak or have a conversation, I know that this is another extension of my brand. I always make an effort to come accross well-versed and educated, afterall I am a branding expert.

With my business cards, they are crisp and precise. They are hardly the most expensive part of my brand, but they always get noticed. People remember them and remember me wherever I travel the world for business or pleasure. They are a reflection of quality that my brand provides.

COST ESTIMATING

I give my new clients a flow chart of the most effective order for creating their brand. I advise them to focus on:

- Corporate identity
- Print media
- Copywriting
- Online presence and search
- Video branding and advertising
- Social media
- PR/Press

These seven areas are inclusive of marketing and branding materials, websites, business cards, and everything else that is most important for establishing a presence that shows you are vested in being a million-dollar brand.

CONSTANTLY REINVEST IN YOUR BRAND

When I first started, I don't know if it was the dumbest or smartest move, but I never took a business loan. My background came from a very old-fashioned dad who didn't believe in borrowing money. That stuck with me. But part of me also felt that if I put in 100%, I would not be able to fail.

> *Being self-made is important to me,*
> *and also how I conduct business.*

This was the route that worked for me. When I assessed my strengths, I knew that I was good at branding, positioning, and making money for clients. I create a vision and am able to see it before it exists. You could say I am a futurist. I've proven it, which is why I've earned the right to tell people what to do if they want to succeed. Anyone who applies themselves properly and isn't lethargic in their efforts has the potential to become a success story.

> *Being self-made is important to me,*
> *and also how I conduct business.*

Million Dollar Branders once did some re-branding work for a chicken company. It was family owned, and they had not done anything for nearly sixty years. This meant that we were not only re-branding but also needed to give the employees excitement about the opportunity

Your brand impacts company morale

For businesses like the chicken company where the staff have uniforms, it is imperative that they wear a uniform they are proud to wear. When they are serving people or in public they represent the brand. They should wear it proudly. Employees should be your biggest fans.

Uniforms are important because they:

- **Identify employees as capable and professional:** Image plays an important role in the way people perceive your business. What your employees wear can have a direct effect on your business. If your employees are sloppy this will effect the success of your brand.

- **Create branding:** When it comes to successfully running a business, any business, it is important to establish a strong brand identity. Uniforms are a part of the branding process, and they work.

> *People ask me about which business's*
> *need branding most. I always answer,*
> *"Only those that want success."*

MAKE $#IT HAPPEN CHECKLIST

✔ **Spend money on the expert first**: Budget is important, yes, but when people are only focused on cost, the message, quality, and experience are the first to go.

✔ **Do not fall into the illusion that "bargain branding" works**: Authentic branding comes with a price, but also generates returns.

✔ **While planning for your business, always plan for branding**: Failing to give a healthy priority to branding and marketing for your business is a costly planning mistake.

✔ **Study cultures and international business**: Learn your potential clients preferred methods, and always be able to precisely state what you represent in five seconds or less.

✔ **Don't shove a bunch of effin' junk at people and expect them to "get you" or "buy you"**: In most cases less is more. Learn your market and what is important to them.

"FAILURES WILL ALWAYS DEFEAT LOSERS AND ALWAYS INSPIRE WINNERS."

Justine P.

JUSTINE P. - FOUNDER - MILLION DOLLAR BRANDERS

FAIL QUICKLY; WIN FASTER

Take it like a Warrior

What are you scared of?

You have to embrace failure to get to where you need to be. I have never been scared of anything in my life—no exaggeration. I'm not sure if it's because I've been around plenty of adversity, that has toughened me up or it's just who I am naturally.

> ### When bad things happen, just say they happened, and move on. Be resilient.

You cannot be scared of going for what you want. Just accept that you've got to put yourself out there. And if things go wrong, accept it. Fail quickly and get it over with. Lesson learned; time to move on.

When I quit my job to start Million Dollar Branders, my dad thought I was crazy. He didn't get it, and he had so many questions, the biggest being: *"How are you going to make money? You're leaving your month to month paycheck to earn nothing and do your own thing"*. He really thought I was nuts...and maybe I was. I was earning a ridiculous salary at the time...but it wasn't my soul purpose in life, and I knew that. I looked at him and said, *"Dad, you know what, I'm going to be good because I have something other people don't have. I have perseverance."*

> **I knew I would never have the opportunity again and if I failed, at least I would know I tried. I would give my best efforts—no exceptions!**

It's been suggested that 98% of people will die without ever achieving their dreams. All I know is that I am not going to be one of those people, and if I'm given the chance, everyone I work with will not be a part of that dismal statistic, either.

Over the years, people have made their judgments about my boldness and fearlessness to pursue what I wanted. I've heard assumptions that I was spoiled, and that my parents handed me everything. Yes, my parents are wonderful and have always helped me as best they could, but I've never asked for anything more than support. The rest, I left up to my initiative and seeking out the people who had taken a journey toward success already.

> **A lot of people have yet to learn that you cannot rely on others for your own success. People don't owe you anything.**

You have to learn what success means to you, without relying on others to hand it to you, or even contribute. Remember, there are a million people doing what you do. Sometimes you will fail, be crap, and have a low day. What are you going to do about it?

> *"It ain't about how hard you hit:*
> *it's about how hard you can get hit.*
> *And keep moving forward. It's how much*
> *you can take, and keep moving forward.*
> *That's how winning is done."*
> **–Rocky Balboa**

You don't need to get hit in the head to learn that lesson.

MILLION DOLLAR MINDSET

Failures don't have to be stifling if you're around people with the right mindset. Anyone—and I mean anyone—who you have in your life that is waiting to either think or say, "I told you so" after you fail, is someone you need to gain distance from as much as possible. Or at least look at them like they're full of $#IT when they talk that way.

Sometimes it's tempting to follow the quick money and take the easy way out. Having the right motivation in your life during these times is essential so you can embrace a "no regrets" policy. One of my friends who started a business had done so after endless, dull job searches that didn't connect him to anything he was excited about. We'd talk and keep each other motivated on occasion, and when we were having those entrepreneurial struggles, we'd build each other up. It made a difference and helped remind me of the good fight I was in, and I was really only in round one.

Then I got a test...

I got offered a job working as a 'User Experience Designer' for a big company, traveling the world, with big perks. It was amazing money and tempting. However, it was easy for me to say "no" because that job went against everything I believed in, which was giving 110% of my efforts to my company with my full heart. Really it wasn't even a question, because I know that I am building something for generations to come.

Did you know most small businesses fail within the first two to five years?

When I started Million Dollar Branders, I was under the impression that I could make my first million dollars in a year. Even with my work ethic, I quickly learned that there were never-ending tasks involved with building a million-dollar business. There were so many trials and tribulations, from accounts to expenses to staff hiring and firing; from clients to new business to great business and bad business. Acknowledging everything would take me longer than a year did not deter me, however. I knew this was my point of difference—I would never give up! I sacrificed blood, sweat, and tears, along with a few moments where I thought I'd perhaps gone insane. But in the end, I knew I would reach success...and then some more. You cannot go wrong when you keep on building and becoming better.

Invest in yourself and your dreams.
Imagine if you spent one hour a day
doing something for yourself to
make you better.

It's sad that so many people give up before success arrives. Just when they are on the verge of a breakthrough, just before that big deal, they run out of gas and don't have the ability to give that extra push that it takes to stick it out. It may be a day away, maybe a month or two, but they just stop. All those efforts wasted. Tough days are something that everyone understands.

So what if you have a crap day.
There are 364 other days besides that
one, so get over it. You have to love
life. Be strong and persevere. In the
end, it will be worth it.

INSPIRATION AND PERSPIRATION OFTEN TEETER ON INSANITY

With my first design job, I was so driven. My vision for myself was big, and I was really tough on myself. I'd never take lunch breaks. I'd stay working, stealing brief glances out the window of where I worked, taking in the beautiful scenery of the ocean. Daylight was foreign to me—I got to work before light and left after it was dark. I was just so desperate to succeed, and no one encouraged me to take a step back and do otherwise.

I had no concept of the benefits of a mental break. One day— finally—someone took notice. Maybe pity, who knows. There was a new Senior Designer, Michelle, and she dragged me from my seat one day and demanded I take a break with her and go for a walk.

On our walk, she told me a story. She mentioned how I was so emotionally attached to my work and she used to be the same way. She'd previously worked for one of the biggest newspapers in New Zealand. She'd do everything she could to make everything look beautiful and perfect. If she had to, she'd sweat it out until 4 or 5 AM, five days a week.

After one of her many big newspaper print runs one day she was walking past the fish and chip shop that was close to the newspaper she worked at. She looked in the window and saw that they were eating fish and chips out of her newspaper. That was when she finally knew she had to have a life and separate herself from her emotional connection to her work.

> ### *It's a big question: what is good for me, and what am I going to get out of this?*

Not living a life with balance is also a failure, and that's what I find is hard for many people to accept. It isn't all one thing or another, but how you manage it all together, as a whole.

MAKE $#IT HAPPEN CHECKLIST

✔ **Don't be narrow-minded**: When we focus so closely on one detail, we lose sight of everything happening around us.

✔ **Write down what scares you most**: This may help you see that your resistance to trying is quite ridiculous.

✔ **Determine which percent you want to be in**: Do you want to be part of the 2% that achieve their dreams or the 98% that live lives based on others' dreams?

✔ **Fail fast**: If you fail—and you will—forgive yourself and move on.

✔ **Value your time**: Time is precious, and wasting it feeling sorry for yourself won't help you or the situation.

"SUCCESS IS 'EFFING EARNED. YOU DIG DOWN DEEP AND GO FOR IT."

Justine P.

JUSTINE P. - FOUNDER - MILLION DOLLAR BRANDERS PTY LTD

LAUNCHING YOUR BUSINESS

Be Fearless in Pursuit of your Dreams

To be direct: don't be a pussy. This applies to everything in your life, but especially in business. You have to have thick skin to launch a business.

Far too many people do not properly launch a business the first time around. As a branding and advertising person, this makes me cringe. You get one first chance. It's up to you to ensure it's done right.

There's no area where people are more peculiar in their actions than in their website. They see their site as the "be all" of their business. Yet, there is nothing saying that five million people are going to look at it for even a second. If you're singular in your focus, time will be wasted, and results will not be delivered.

For anything I am involved in launching, I have a staunch rule: I will not launch a half product or in a haphazard manner. Taking my time and making sure things are absolutely on point and impactful is a signature mark of the services that Million Dollar Branders offers. This goes against the grain for many people but has proven itself to be a winning formula. Haphazard may get some results, but they are luck. I'm a creative strategist, and this is a more reliable commodity to have.

Launching your business means you must get people to be vested in an experience and perception. Launching your business means you must get people to be vested in an experience and perception. You 3-5 seconds to make a lasting impression. You could have the most stunning clothes and accessories in the market for your price range, but if your brand and experience is $#it you'll still lose 99% of customers.

If you choose a $5 logo, you're showing a $5 product. How do you expect to get paid big money?

The best doesn't always cost the most, but it is customized to what you need to properly brand a business, so it launches properly. This is why successful people don't just wake up one morning and say, *"Hey, I'm going to open up a business today. I'll be rich tomorrow."* You need to invest time, ideas, and money. You must find the right people and training to help you build.

Building a million dollar brand requires patience, persistance and energy.

At Million Dollar Branders, we specialize in making a brand look like it's been around for a long time, we also make it look "expensive" even if it is launching for the first time. We know how important it is to create raving fans.

Regardless of if you're launching a new invention or an improved version of something people know, you can show that you're operating at an elite level,that you believe in your product and its potential. It will ultimately attract the clients you want and need.

MAKE $#IT HAPPEN CHECKLIST

✔ **Don't do a half job**: You must be a perfectionist because not doing your best is laziness.

✔ **Be aggressive and fearless in your launch**: Bring in experts and give yourself a good chance for success.

✔ **Logo, branding, website, and image all need to make sense**: They should be a cohesive package.

✔ **Interview 5 of your ideal clients**: Ask the types of people you wish to do business with what they think of your business model before you launch. You don't have to listen to all feedback, but you should be smart enough to take constructive criticism and recognize any gaps that are pointed out.

✔ **Create a checklist**: This allows you to visually see that everything is prepared for your most successful launch efforts.

"BRAND YOURSELF IN A WAY THAT PEOPLE WILL PAY FOR YOU."

Justine P.

JUSTINE P. - FOUNDER - MILLION DOLLAR BRANDERS PTY LTD

JE NE SAIS QUOI: AN INTANGIBLE QUALITY THAT MAKES SOMETHING DISTINCTIVE OR ATTRACTIVE.

WITH SOME X-FACTOR ON TOP.

Justine P.

JUSTINE P. - FOUNDER - MILLION DOLLAR BRANDERS PTY LTD

YES, IMAGE MATTERS

Be a Vision of the Success You Seek

How you look matters. This fact may not be convenient or fall into the insight you hear about your self-worth not being attached to your image, and that's fine. But be cautioned—your business results are definitely tied into your image.

Would you go to a dentist with terrible teeth?

How about getting a manicure from someone whose nails were bitten to the skin?

Do you purchase your dream Lamborghini from a dealer or from a guy who is driving a twenty-year-old rust bucket?

Our image is associated with five main areas:

1. **The way we dress**: A polished image is important when you are attending events where you are representing your brand. If you are the face of your business, you should always be ready to present, pitch, and create connections. This doesn't

mean you have to dress in the most expensive clothes, but they should fit properly, be clean and pressed, and be professional. For guys—those pants that hang below your butt need to be thrown out. Ladies—don't make the focal point of your audience's attention the gap in your blouse that exposes your cleavage. How you dress in a corporate meeting can sometimes be the difference between signing a $1k deal or $50k deal. The way you dress impacts the way you make $#it happen.

2. **The manner in which we speak**: Whether your product is an individual service you offer or the product of your company, you need to be a professional spokesperson. Vulgar and offensive language may offend the people you need most—whether they are right in front of you or overhear you. When you walk away, you want people to murmur about how impressed they are with you, not about how shocking your behavior is.

3. **The way we carry ourselves**: Our body language says a great deal about our confidence in whom we are, which transcends to the business we conduct. If you cannot look someone in the eyes, work on correcting this. Be aware of what your presence is saying about you.

4. **Our self-care**: Grooming is necessary. Don't go from sweating like a pig from that much-needed workout into a business meeting smelling like you bathed in sweat. Pay attention to your breath, your makeup, not having too much cologne on, not smelling like smoke if you're a smoker and all the details that may turn off the people you are in a crowd with. Nail biting can also be a deal breaker. Admit it...you know that you

can't stand those things in other people so pay attention to your self-care.

5. **Don't be a know-it-all**: Know-it-all's who have opinions about everything are annoyng to be around, and people will find a way to gravitate away from them. If you don't know the art of having a good conversation, learn it. It'll serve you well in every area of your life. Take a 5/1 rule—for every five minutes you give them, take thirty seconds to talk about yourself. it sounds easy, but it's not. It takes practice and skill. Simon Senek's view on being the last to speak is extremely powerful:

"If you agree with somebody, dont nod yes,
if you disagree with somebody don't nod no.

You will be told your whole life that you need to learn to listen. I would say that you need to be the last to speak. To hold your opinions to yourself does two things:
1.) Is the feeling that they have been heard. It gives everyone else the feeling that they have contributed.
2.)You get the benefit of hearing what everybody else has to think before you render your opinion."

Our image is quickly summarized by the people we meet in an instant. Be someone that people want to know. Your image is a very effective sales tool for the opportunities you'll receive—or not receive.

MAKE $#IT HAPPEN CHECKLIST

✔ **Understand what your clothing says about you**: If you are unsure of this on your own, work with an image consultant or stylist that can show you how. Remember smelling good is just as important as looking good!

✔ **Speak and interact appropriately**: Speak in a polished manner. Always be mindful of maintaining a good distance between you and who you are talking to. You never want to invade anyone's bubble. This type of behavior is just as awful as it is awkward.

✔ **Become attuned to your body language**: Body language and how you physically express yourself are two forms of communication. It is often more powerful than your words.

✔ **Spell check emails and letters**: This is another reflection and extension of you and your business. These types of errors are often associated with laziness and being unprofessional.

"BE TRUTHFUL WITH YOURSELF. SET YOURSELF IMPOSSIBLE GOALS. THIS IS HOW YOU SUPRISE YOURSELF AND IGNITE KILLER SUCCESS AND MAKE EPIC $#IT HAPPEN."

Justine P.

JUSTINE P. - FOUNDER - MILLION DOLLAR BRANDERS PTY LTD

YOUR NETWORK IS YOUR NET WORTH
Know People Who Know Business

Chances are, you at least know a friend of a friend who has done a great job at something. Don't hesitate to approach them first. You never know when you'll come across someone who has what you've been missing. These types of networking opportunities can help your business grow exponentially faster.

Of course, then you also must know how to network.

You can go to a great network group, and if you're a $#IT networker, you'll get nothing out of it. If you were to go to a network function and find yourself crippled and unable to get any value from it, you need to take that "oh 'ef'" moment seriously. From that moment on, start doing something you're uncomfortable with every day to get over the hurdle of talking to other people about your business, and also learning about theirs. John Mcgrath, Australian entreprenur and real estate mogul said it nicely when he explained at a conference - everyday take yourself out of your comfort zone for 60 seconds - push yourself to do something brave. This will elevate your success.

If you don't know how to network, get out of your comfort zone and learn how.

If you cannot break through and network effectively, you need to determine who you have around that can be a driving force for what you are doing. You need this person on your team if you can't fill the role—no exceptions.

Despite being shy when I was younger—so shy I could barely open my mouth in a classroom—I've learned that I have a natural way of doing this when I'm around people. It began by finding things that were of interest to me about other people and grew from there. Today, it is not a problem. Remember that it is always about "them," and never about you. The same is true when building a brand.

Good networkers give the person they are talking to 'five minutes of fame'. They are remembered.

Whenever you end a conversation at a networking event, you want to feel like the person you were speaking with received value from the conversation. This will make it easier for them to remember you.

MAKE $#IT HAPPEN CHECKLIST

✔ **Finesse your networking skills**: Evaluate your abilities and work toward improvements where necessary. Take changes you have nothing to lose.

✔ **Understand how to engage someone in a conversation**: Being mindful of body language, tone, and presence while you converse with people will lead to the best interactions.

✔ **Have a powerful 'elevator pitch'**: This pitch is your secret weapon. It should be short and sweet (10-15 seconds or less). The sharper your pitch, the sharper the business deal you close.

✔ **Work on your memory**: Nothing blows it more than asking the same person repeatedly at different events what their name is. Be one step ahead.

✔ **Take advantage of your people resources**: Those who know you and recognize you're a high-quality individual will not hesitate to refer you to others that can help you, or that you can help.

"ONLY YOU DETERMINE THE LEGACY YOU LEAVE BEHIND."

Justine P.

JUSTINE P. · FOUNDER · MILLION DOLLAR BRANDERS™

THE HUMAN TOUCH

Attitude, Drive, & Charisma = Always Be Closing

Attitude, drive, and charisma are three qualities that are a part of my personality that I've committed to mastering. Some of the skills are natural, and others have been focused on until I mastered them. Many people don't have these things naturally, but they can be developed. These qualities are an important part of real branding and can be used to create stellar products that deliver everything they are designed to be to consumers. However, if you—the face of the product—don't match the brand, there's a problem. You'll need to work on being better.

ATTITUDE

A great business person is confident, humble and not arrogant. It doesn't matter how much money you make or what you do always remember the foundations of your career.

Jack Delosa—successful entrepreneur and Founder of The Entourage, Australia made his first 25 million at 27 years of age.

Jack learnt about attitude at a young age. He says *"As your success grows so should your humility"*.

Not thinking you know everything is significant. Remember who helped you and where you come from. It's a part of your story. With branding, people often forget where they came from when they get to the top. As you rise, remember where you came from and the supporting crew or dream team that helped. This is how you begin to create your legacy.

DRIVE

Drive relates to knowing that you are prepared to put in all the necessary effort to **earn** your success. You have to be willing to put in the hard yards. If you're not, you have a problem.

You can't sit on your butt and make things happen. You will never achieve a millionaire status simply by wanting it, but not putting forth any efforts to obtain it. You have to want it—and act on it. It's not one or the other; it's a combination of both. It doesn't' matter if you're a bus driver or work in a donut shop. You must have the drive and give 100%. Yes, you may get tired, but your attitude will help you keep your drive because you understand that you'll get further in life.

My drive is one of my greatest strengths because it allows me to stay positive and focused when I'm challenged. I work my way around whatever tries to jam me up, even when it isn't easy. However, when it gets to be too much, you should take a break and recharge with something healthy, and then get back at it.

Your drive should be clear to clients If you don't go a step further, someone else will. Why touch something and put your name on it if you're not driven to ensure it is amazing?

One last note about drive—Most people do not realize the drive it took for successful people to get where they are. So much hard work is put into a business or idea before most people even know it exists. Anthony Robbins says it perfectly *"People are rewarded in public for what they practice for years in private."*

CHARISMA

Charisma is a quality that has different meanings and interpretations to different people. When it comes to branding your product, or yourself, you need to be authentic. You also need to know your target customer. What is charismatic to one person may not be to another. However, the qualities of a good, engaged, and intelligent person often show through despite personal tastes.

For me, my charisma starts with the way I'm thinking in a specific moment and carries on through to the way I dress and enter into a room. I am always dressed with a million-dollar mindset. Do I pay a million dollars for my clothes? No, but they are an important part of the overall impression.

Some people believe certain brand names are classy because of the label, nothing more. However, if you put on a brand name label and have chewed up nails, a bad dye job, and old scuffed up shoes on you are hardly classy. That's just a fact, folks. As they say, "You can put lipstick on a pig, but it's still a pig." Wear what looks good on you and flatters you. Dress for success.

Charisma isn't pretending to be someone you're not, either, but being the best version of your authentic self.

> *"Truly charismatic people, in my experience, don't come along very often."*
> **—Francesca Annis**

If everyone were charismatic, no one would be charismatic. Charisma can add another 'o' to any business deal. It is an extremely valuable trait.

However, if you have big plans and goals and know you are lacking charisma, how do you get it? Try growing comfortable with some of these suggestions:

- **Understand your space and 'presence'.** (Learn from some historic icons by reading, and watch them on YouTube e.g Kennedy, Coco Chanel, Barack Obama...the list goes on).

- **Always give before you receive**, Knowing you may never receive. Serving is the only way to establish a real connection and relationship.

- **Be humble and authentic.** Make it about the people you are around, NOT about YOU. No one likes a stuffy, pretentious, self-important person.

- **Be confident but NOT arrogant.** Confidence is a secret magnet that naturally attracts people to you.

- **Shine the spotlight on others.** No one receives enough praise. Tell people what they did well. Place emphasis on their achievements.

- **Be articulate and listen much more than you speak.** Choose your words carefully. Words are powerful and have an effect on those around you.

- **Dress for success.** Always look classy, elegant and neat.

- **Don't ever discuss the failings of others**. Readily admit your own failings. Choose your attitude carefully.

- **Remember: ADC = ABC**
(Attitude Drive Charisma = Always Be Closing)

MAKE $#IT HAPPEN CHECKLIST

✔ **Ask for what you deserve with confidence**: You'll be surprised how wonderfully this works.

✔ **Manage your energy well**: Whenever you feel so exhausted that you're ready to park your drive, pull over and fuel up so you can get going again. You always need your drive.

✔ **Attitude alert**: If your attitude sucks, your results will too.

✔ **Develop strategies to up your charisma**: Determine what areas you lack charisma in and set up an improvement plan to conquer them.

✔ **Wake up and embrace a success mindset**: When you wake up every day assume that you're going to get an opportunity for a BIG opportunity and be prepared for it. Before you leave the house, make sure you look like a million dollars and have the 'million dollar' business cards to match. You'll be suprised how your day turns out.

"FOLLOW YOUR GUT.
STAND UP FOR
WHAT IS RIGHT,
EVEN IF YOU STAND
ALONE."

Justine P.

JUSTINE P. - FOUNDER - MILLION DOLLAR BRANDERS PTY LTD

DEAR MILLENNIALS

Dear Millennials,

Look, I get it; it's not easy being you and part of a generation that is full of people who "have it now". Then there are the complainers (parents, teachers, expectations), always nagging you. They say you have a self-absorbed nature; that you just don't get it, that you are lazy, entitled etc. It's frustrating and NOT easy to tune that crap out.

Maybe life's been really easy for you, or maybe it hasn't been. Either way - you need to realise that you're responsible for the outcomes in your own life. I believe in you. I believe it is your time to shine! It's time to know your want, your why and your purpose. To make an impact.Your potential to excel in this fast moving world is endless.

Have you ever heard of Richard Branson? He's the billionaire who knows how to relate to you guys better than just about every other mega-wealthy man out there. When he was a kid, he wasn't the best in school (he couldn't even spell) or the most popular. In fact, he struggled, but you know what he had? Confidence. How about you? If your mom dropped you off in the woods, six miles from your home, what would you do? Would you hunker down and cry, or find your way back home and navigate the big world in front of you confidently? Richard's mum actually did that, and he made it. It taught him a great lesson about determination and ability. I'm not saying this basic adventure will elevate you to his status, but it goes to show you that any damn thing you set out to do, regardless of your age, is possible. The only thing that stops you is excuses.

Dream big... Hopefully, you have dreams, as they are wonderful. And it's the craziest thing, you know, they can come true. There is only one thing that says they cannot come true. What is it? It's you. If you don't take action and kick it into gear, you aren't going to achieve much, regardless of how kind and amazing and "smart" you are.

Sure, things are a bit crazy in this world. People are nuts; many seem so cruel. Others just don't "get you," and you just don't know how to explain yourself to them so that they do. In fact, it's not worth the bother. It's too bad, really, because you are filled with ideas that really might make a difference. Why haven't you pursued them? If you can be certain of one thing, it is that no one else will pursue them for you. For themselves, maybe, but not you. It isn't happening.

It's not always easy to be confident in a world where you are instantly judged by the way you look or act, but you're not the first generation to have this happen to them. It's always been the case. Elvis's sexy hip swivels made parents faint, thinking their daughters were going to hell just for screaming about it. Every growing generation is faced with criticism—you're not an original in that way. But you are capable of changing the world. You are capable of absolutely anything you put your mind to.

I hate to be harsh with you. Wait, actually I don't. I need to be. There is no person in this world that's going to give you the life you want aside from the one that you see in your selfie. It's time to gain some perspective.

Work toward what you want. Your life's purpose. Live your dream.

Desire achieving what you want yourself. If you get something for free, that means it has no value, right? Smiles and rainbows are free and pretty great, but if you're looking down at everything you probably won't look up and notice them. So...

Really, I just want you to know that your day has come. I have faith that you can do "anything" for a lot of reasons. First, "anything" is a vague term, which leaves the entire world at your disposal. Second, you are a person, which means you have gifts and challenges both. Third, you define your success, and no one else. This means that it's up to you. That should be a relief.

So, what do you say? I say it's time to get your a$$ out there and get $#IT done! Show the world what your made of. Make an impact, GO BIG or go home! You guys are secretly my favourite - because the world is your oyster.

Sincerely,

Justine P.

A Get $#IT Done Expert

"BIG REWARDS
ARE GIVEN
TO BIG
DREAMERS".

Justine P.

JUSTINE P. - FOUNDER - MILLION DOLLAR BRANDERS PTYLTD

DEAR BURNT OUT

Dear Burnt Out,

Are you ready for something else? I don't blame you. You've maybe been spending a whole lot of years and energy contributing to someone else's dream, all while ignoring your own. It's easy to assume that you don't like it, and you want something different, but you're stuck. Maybe even a bit numb.

These crisis moments are taxing. No one wants to feel like a pile of dung has taken up residency right on top of your very spirit for living. I get it, and it can happen as life happens. The ambitions and energy you once had to make your way in this world grew awry. Dreams were put aside for families. A steady paycheck replaced the exhilaration of a bit of risk. But you did promise yourself "some day."

And I'll be damned, "some day" did come and with it came technology and new generations with endless energy and an understanding of the newer, fast-paced world. Suddenly you felt out of place. But know this—this world is just as much yours as it is the Millennials or any other generation. You can experience more things than ever today if you choose to do it.

Maybe it's time for you to step up and regain a bit of control. It's completely in your capable, experienced hands. You, too, can do wild things and give yourself a revolution of thought and action by grabbing onto those lost dreams or connecting with new dreams you have yet to explore. Does it sound tough? Probably, because it can be. Not as tough as living through feeling like you're in a never-ending state of emergency, though. Or waking up and wondering "what now."

It's time to get over whatever has been going on and get going! You've learned a lot of $#IT over the years, and a lot of what you know is pretty damn valuable. Believe it. It's true. And somewhere in your brain, behind the haze created by your "must dos" is the "want to dos" and they are waiting. Blow off the dust and start doing, already.

You know what? I believe you're up to a good challenge—one that will invigorate your senses and kick your drive into gear. Instead of thinking your best days have passed you by and your opportunities are dried up, go for a new approach. Believe this adamantly and vigorously: today is the best opportunity you've had so far. It is, but it's up to you to decide what you are going to do with it.

Boss up and take control. You can become fulfilled at any age, and there is no age limit on living your passions.

Think about what you want, and then take action. That's how you get $#IT done!

It's finally your time to shine, so don't keep wasting away.

Sincerely,

Justine P.

A Regret Free Life and Get $#IT Done Expert

"YOU CAN'T DO EPICLY GREAT $#IT WITH BASIC PEOPLE."

Justine P.

JUSTINE P. - FOUNDER - MILLION DOLLAR BRANDERS PTY LTD

RESOURCES PAGE

Below is a list of entrepreneur and business owner-centric websites that each contain great content to help you better understand and conduct business. They will give you the million dollar mindset that my clients take on when they establish their million dollar brand.

Don't let your own limits define you.
You are responsible for your own
destiny. Make $#it happen. TODAY.

Connect with Million Dollar Branders

(f) **milliondollarbranders**

(○) **milliondollarbranders**

(in) **milliondollarbranders**

(▶) **milliondollarbranders**

ForEntrepreneurs.com

OneVest.com

AudienceBloom.com

Dutiee.com

Quora.com

AngelList.com

EpicLaunch.com

BusinessOwnersToolkit.com

ChicCEO.com

AllBusiness.com

ForteFoundation.com

Medium.com

TheBossNetwork.org

ASmartBear.com

StartupCompanyLawyer.com

EscapeFromCubicleNation.com

BrazenLife.com

AllThingsD.com

VentureBlog.com

Reddit: startups

CopyBlogger.com

CrunchBase.com

Entrepreneur.com

500Hats.com

FTC.gov

HBR.org

News.YCombinator.com

KISSmetrics.com

Microsoft.com

Noobpreneur.com

Mixergy.com

MarieForleo.com

SBA.gov

QuickSprout.com

Score.org

SaaStr.com

TheStartupDonut.com

StartupMeme.com

TED.com

TheFunded.com

Boss.blogs.nytimes.com

Blog.guykawasaki.com

YourSuccessNow.com

Under30CEO.com

Marco.org

StartupDigest.com

Innerpreneur.com

TheEconomist.com

Inc.com

Forbes.com

Grammarly.com

Entrepornography.com

Webdesignerdepot.com

Pinterest.com

Adsoftheworld.com

Awwwards.com

Nytimes.com

Entrepornography.com

Evernote.com

Milliondollarbranders.com

MY GIFT TO YOU

For my whole life, my core value system has been to help people to step into their true power, bring out their light, live their purpose, OWN IT and believe that they are capable of anything they put their mind to.

If you have a friend or family member who <u>you</u> think needs some help to make $#IT happen go to our shop:

www.milliondollarbranders.com/shop

At the checkout, you'll be prompted to put your lucky loved ones name in the delivery spot along with the code: **GIFTMEMDB** at checkout and they will receive a FREE 'Make $#it Happen' book in the mail. All you need to do is pay for postage and handling.

Enjoy! and keep making $#it happen.

Sincerely,

Justine P.

SHARE YOUR SUCCESS

I would love to hear about your success stories, and how this book has impacted your life and helped you to make $#it happen. I'm open to answering any questions BIG or small. Let's connect!

Email me directly at: **justinep@milliondollarbranders.com**
web: **www.milliondollarbranders.com**

Here's to BIG things and Making $#it Happen!

Love,

Justine P.

"GO BIG OR GO HOME."

Justine P.

JUSTINE P. - FOUNDER - MILLION DOLLAR BRANDERS PTY LTD

END NOTES

1   Why 8% of Sales People Get 80% of the Sales. Clay, Robert of Marketing Donut. http://www.marketingdonut.co.uk/sales/sales-techniques-and-negotiations/why-8-of-sales-people-get-80-of-the-sales. Extracted on 4/17/17.

2   Ridiculous Stats that Will Make You Realize How Much Time You Waste in Life. Bussmann, Caitlyn. October 19, 2015. http://www.rantnow.com/2015/10/19/ridiculous-stats-that-will-make-you-realize-how-much-time-you-waste-in-life/. Extracted on 4/18/17.

3   20 Statistics about Branding Every Entrepreneur and Marketer Should Know. Kimbarovsky, Arielle. January 20, 2017. https://blog.crowdspring.com/2017/01/successful-branding-for-entrepreneurs-statistics/. Extracted on 4/30/17.

4   Apple Facts and Statistics. Smith, Craig. April 25, 2017. http://expandedramblings.com/index.php/by-the-numbers-amazing-apple-stats. Extracted on 5/2/17.

5   Humans have shorter attention span than goldfish, thanks to smartphones. Watson, Leon. May 15, 2015. Telegraph. http://www.telegraph.co.uk/science/2016/03/12/humans-have-shorter-attention-span-than-goldfish-thanks-to-smart. Extracted on 5/3/17.

6   Attention Span Statistics. Statistic Brain. National Center for Biotechnology Information, U.S. National Library of Medicine, The Associated Press. July 2, 2016. http://www.statisticbrain.com/attention-span-statistics/. Extracted on 5/1/17.

7   Source: Harald Weinreich, Hartmut Obendorf, Eelco Herder, and Matthias Mayer: "Not Quite the Average: An Empirical Study of Web Use," in the ACM Transactions on the Web, vol. 2, no. 1 (February 2008), article #5. Extracted on 5/1/17.

8   How Uniforms Boost Team Morale and Your Company Image. Jet Uniform & Supply Blog. February 16, 2015. http://www.jetuniform. com/blog/2015/02/how-uniforms-boost-team-morale-and-your-companys-image/. Extracted on 5/22/17.